SOUTHERN
HEIRLOOM COOKING

SOUTHERN HEIRLOOM COOKING

200 TREASURED FEEL-GOOD RECIPES

NORMA JEAN McQUEEN HAYDEL
AND HORACE MCQUEEN

Good Books

New York, New York

Good Books books may be purchased in bulk at special discounts for sales promotion, corporate gifts, fund-raising, or educational purposes. Special editions can also be created to specifications. For details, contact the Special Sales Department, Good Books, 307 West 36th Street, 11th Floor, New York, NY 10018 or info@skyhorsepublishing.com.

Good Books is an imprint of Skyhorse Publishing, Inc.®, a Delaware corporation.

Visit our website at www.goodbooks.com.

10 9 8 7 6 5 4 3 2

Library of Congress Cataloging-in-Publication Data is available on file.

Cover design by Laura Klynstra

Print ISBN: 978-1-68099-131-4
Ebook ISBN: 978-1-68099-142-0

Printed in China

TABLE OF CONTENTS

About Southern Heirloom Cooking

For years, my husband, three sons, and grandchildren have asked me to write down my recipes so that they can make their favorite foods and have the recipes to pass along to the next generations. This is a great compliment to my cooking, but I haven't found it easy to record the recipes. You see, I don't cook a dish the same way every time I make it. I may add something one time or take something away the next time.

My cooking has never been something that I *had* to do—it has always been something I enjoy and take great pride in. Mostly it's my imagination working, along with a pinch of this and a little of that. My greatest feeling of accomplishment is when my family and friends let go with the "Ooh's" and "Aah's" and "Please tell me how you cooked that!"

When I was a child, my mother, after much argument, let me cook lunch one day, all by myself and unsupervised. I will never forget the experience. She bragged on me, which made me very proud. And from then on, she let me experiment in the kitchen whenever I wanted. Recipes seemed to get in my way, so I would imagine what I wanted to create. I loved dreaming up dishes, experimenting with creating them, and then discovering that other people liked them, too.

After I married my husband Joe and started a family, I was able to stay at home for several years while my sons, Richie, Cliff, and Gordon, were growing up. I used recipes given to me by my mother, grandmother, and aunts, as well as recipes from Joe's family. While my family ate traditional Southern food, Joe's family cooked with a Louisiana Cajun flavor. His mother, Josephine Morvaunt Haydel, was raised on a sugar cane plantation and was a very good cook. Joe enjoyed the spicier dishes his mother cooked, so I did my best to do justice to them. I learned to be more creative in my use of seasonings.

My sons are now grown and are all married to wonderful women. And I've learned more dishes from them! In fact, some of the recipes that I'm sharing in this collection are ones that we've all learned to love from my daughters-in-law.

I am sixty-eight years old and still experimenting with food. I get such satisfaction and enjoyment when I succeed. For the last four years I have tried to remember to measure my ingredients when I cook. Many of the following recipes are in this family collection because I did remember to measure—and then write down what I did! You may want to add or subtract to your own taste, but the basic information is what's important. I hope you enjoy all of these favorite recipes of ours.

—*Norma Jean McQueen Haydel*

I am Norma Jean's youngest sibling, so I've enjoyed her cooking for a lot of years. My mom and sisters, as well as my two brothers, were all good in the kitchen. Being surrounded by such great cooks made me want to try my hand at making food, too.

My parents had seven children. On top of that, my father was not well during most of my childhood. Looking after us and after him took a lot of my mother's time. Instant mixes and modern appliances were not a part of our life, so Mom did all of her cooking from scratch. But she did that everyday cooking with care and love.

My earliest assignment in the kitchen was to help with the dishes after a meal had been cooked and served. The only cooking I was permitted to do in those years was on Boy Scout camp-outs.

When I was a teenager, I worked with my oldest brother on a charter fishing boat in Biloxi, Mississippi. He was a wizard at cooking the seafood that he brought home from his fishing trips. He let me experiment, and I learned a lot about cooking from him.

As important, I saw how much pleasure it gave him to create a meal that everyone enjoyed. Much of my interest in and appreciation of cooking stems from watching the joy it gave him.

When my wife, Carleen, and I first married, neither of us had much experience cooking. Carleen came from a farming family in east Texas and grew up eating Southern country cooking. But we learned by tackling the recipes our families and friends gave to us. And we discovered how to adapt them to suit our tastes.

As in many Southern families, our children, Greg, Denise, and Melissa, often threw their hands up in frustration at our inability to give them exact measurements in a "handed-down" recipe. When one of them would ask, "How much of this or that?", we would answer as best we could—"A pinch," or "Until it looks (or tastes) right." Now that they are grown up and on their own, we've made an effort to write down the recipe measurements they need. Those family favorites are in this book.

One more thing. I have come to believe—out of necessity, you understand!—that an essential ingredient in cooking is a sense of humor. Not everything I've cooked has turned out as I had imagined it should, and my family always finds a way to let me know when it hasn't! But after years of having family and friends share recipes and honest advice with me, I am confident enough to do more than fire up the grill. I'm now getting my share of "Aah's," and you will, too, with these recipes!

— Horace McQueen

Appetizers and Snacks

ANGELS ON HORSEBACK

Makes 6–8 servings

24 shucked oysters
¼ cup lemon juice
1 tsp. Worcestershire sauce
3 dashes hot sauce
12 slices bacon
wooden toothpicks

1. Place oysters in a bowl and add lemon juice, Worcestershire sauce, and hot sauce. Stir to coat oysters with the sauce.
2. Cut each bacon slice in half and wrap each half slice around an oyster. Secure with a toothpick.
3. Place oysters on a rack in baking pan. Either broil for 3 minutes on each side, or bake in a 350°F oven for about 8 minutes. They are done when the bacon slice is crisp.

Notes:
   1. These are even better grilled. Place the oysters in a grill basket and grill over medium hot coals for about 4 minutes on each side.
   2. Devils on Horseback are pitted prunes stuffed with almonds (or olives), wrapped in bacon, and broiled until crisp.

ARMADILLO EGGS

Yields 15 eggs

1 lb. Monterey Jack cheese
½ lb. bulk sausage
1½ cups buttermilk baking mix
15 canned whole, medium-sized jalapeño peppers
1 box Shake & Bake for pork
2 eggs, beaten

1. Grate half the cheese. Cube the remaining half into fifteen pieces.
2. Mix together grated cheese, sausage, and baking mix. This will make a very stiff dough and should be kneaded for several minutes. Set aside.
3. Slit and seed the peppers. Stuff each pepper with a cube of cheese; then pinch the pepper closed around the cheese.
4. Pinch off a bit of the sausage mixture and pat into a flat circle, about ¼-inch thick. Place cheese-stuffed pepper in the middle of the circle. Wrap each pepper completely with a circle of dough, forming an egg-shaped piece. Make sure all edges are sealed.
5. Roll each "egg" in the Shake & Bake mix until well coated. Dip in the beaten eggs and again in the Shake & Bake mix.
6. Bake in a preheated 300°F oven for 20–25 minutes. The "eggs" will be soft when removed from the oven but will turn crusty as they cool.

ARTICHOKE CHEESE SQUARES

Makes about 20 squares

⅓ cup onion, chopped fine
1 small clove garlic, chopped
2 Tbsp. butter or margarine
4 eggs, well beaten
14 oz. can artichoke hearts, drained and finely chopped
¼ cup dry bread crumbs
½ lb. Swiss or cheddar cheese, shredded
2 Tbsp. minced parsley
¼ tsp. salt
¼ tsp. oregano
¼ tsp. black pepper
¼ tsp. hot pepper sauce

1. Sauté onion and garlic in butter.
2. Mix eggs, artichokes, bread crumbs, cheese, parsley, seasonings, and hot pepper sauce. Add onions and garlic.
3. Turn into buttered 11" x 7" x 1" pan.
4. Bake at 325°F for 30 minutes or until set. Cut into squares.

HOT ARTICHOKE DIP

Makes about 2½ cups

14 oz. can artichokes, broken up into pieces
½ cup mayonnaise
4 oz. can chopped green chiles
1 cup grated Parmesan cheese

1. Combine all ingredients and bake in a shallow four-cup baking dish for 15 minutes at 350°F.
2. Serve with crackers.

<< Hot Artichoke Dip

BACON CHESTNUTS

Makes about 40 chestnuts

1 lb. bacon
3 8 oz. cans whole water chestnuts
½ cup brown sugar
½ cup ketchup

1. Cut bacon strips in half. Wrap a piece of uncooked bacon around each chestnut and secure with a toothpick.
2. Place on baking sheet and bake at 350°F for about 35 minutes or until bacon is crisp. Drain.
3. In another bowl, mix brown sugar and ketchup. Pour over chestnuts. Bake another 20 minutes. Serve hot.

CHEESE DIP IN BREAD

Makes about 3½ cups

10 oz. cheddar cheese, grated
2 cups mayonnaise
1 medium onion, chopped fine
½ tsp. chili powder
1 large round loaf of bread

1. Place all ingredients, except bread, in the top of a double boiler. Heat on low, stirring occasionally.
2. Cut the center out of the bread loaf. Tear the removed bread into small pieces.
3. When the cheese has melted and the dip is smooth and hot, pour the dip inside the loaf and use the small pieces of bread as dippers.

MARINATED BEEF JERKY

Years ago, meat was preserved by salting it, pickling it, or drying it. Dried game and dried beef were called "jerky." Meat from the front quarters of the animal was cut into strips; then salted and peppered and hung in the sun or over a smoking fire until all its moisture was removed. The following recipe tells you how to dry jerky in the oven. It makes a great snack.

1¼ cups lemon juice
1 Tbsp. salt
1 Tbsp. pepper
1 Tbsp. oregano, crushed
1 small green pepper, minced
2 cups water
2 lb. round steak

1. Bring all ingredients (except meat) to a boil and then remove from heat. Cool.
2. Cut meat into strips, each about 6 inches long, 2 inches wide, and ¾ inch thick.
3. Pour the cooled mixture over the meat strips. Marinate for 8 hours in the refrigerator.
4. Remove meat from marinade and lay strips across a broiling pan.
5. Put into a cold oven and turn oven to lowest setting. Let the meat dry in the oven at this temperature for 10–12 hours. Cool completely.
6. The meat will not need to be refrigerated when it is completely dry. Store it in a covered container.

CHEESE SURPRISES

Makes about 2 dozen pieces

1 stick (¼ lb.) margarine
½ lb. cheddar cheese, grated
¼–½ tsp. hot sauce
dash garlic salt
1½ cups flour
about 24 medium-sized stuffed olives

1. Have margarine and cheese at room temperature.
2. Blend margarine, cheese, hot sauce, and garlic salt together with fingertips.
3. Add flour gradually and blend well until dough forms.
4. Break off small bits of dough and flatten in the palm of your hand, using just enough to wrap completely around an olive.
5. Bake on an ungreased cookie sheet at 350°F for about 15 minutes.

CHILE CHEESE STRAWS

Makes about 2½–3 dozen straws

2 cups (8 oz.) Monterey Jack cheese, shredded
½ cup butter or margarine, softened
1 cup all-purpose flour
½ cup yellow cornmeal
1 tsp. chili powder
½ tsp. salt
½ tsp. ground cumin

1. Combine cheese and butter until well blended.
2. Gradually add remaining ingredients, stirring until mixture is no longer crumbly and will shape into a ball.
3. Use a cookie press fitted with a star-shaped disk to shape dough into straws. Or divide dough into four pieces of equal size, roll each portion into a ¼-inch thick rectangle on waxed paper, and cut 2″ x ½″ strips with a knife or pastry wheel.
4. Lay strips on an ungreased baking sheet and bake at 375°F for 8 minutes or until lightly browned.

FRIED CHEESE

Makes 6 servings

½ lb. mozzarella cheese
1 egg
2 Tbsp. water
½ cup seasoned bread crumbs
4 Tbsp. vegetable oil

1. Slice cheese into $\frac{1}{3}$-inch thick pieces.
2. Break egg into a shallow dish, add water and beat well.
3. Pour seasoned bread crumbs onto a plate.
4. Heat oil in a heavy skillet.
5. Dip cheese slices into egg and then into bread crumbs, coating well. Fry slices in hot oil, turning once, until both sides are nicely browned.

CHILE RELLENOS SQUARES

Makes 12 squares

2 eggs
6 egg whites
¼ cup all-purpose flour
½ tsp. baking powder
1 cup cottage cheese
¼ cup grated cheddar cheese
¼ cup grated Monterey Jack cheese
4 oz. can chopped green chiles
½ tsp. hot sauce

1. In a small bowl, beat eggs and egg whites lightly. Add flour and baking powder.
2. Combine remaining ingredients in a separate bowl.
3. Stir in egg mixture.
4. Pour into an 8-inch square greased baking pan.
5. Bake at 400°F for 10 minutes. Reduce heat to 350°F and bake for 35 minutes more. Cut into twelve squares and serve warm.

COWBOY CAVIAR

Makes 8–10 servings

15 oz. can black beans, rinsed and drained
4 oz. can chopped ripe olives, drained
¼ cup chopped onion
1 clove garlic, finely chopped
2 Tbsp. vegetable oil
2 Tbsp. lime juice
¼ tsp. salt
¼ tsp. cayenne pepper
¼ tsp. ground cumin
¼ tsp. black pepper
8 oz. pkg. cream cheese, at room temperature
2 hard-cooked eggs, chopped
1 green onion, chopped
15 oz. pkg. tortilla chips

1. Mix all ingredients together except cream cheese, eggs, onion, and chips.
2. Cover and refrigerate at least two hours.
3. Spread cream cheese on serving plate.
4. Spoon bean mixture evenly over cream cheese.
5. Arrange eggs over bean mixture in ring around edge of plate.
6. Sprinkle with onion.
7. Serve with tortilla chips.

HOT CRABMEAT DIP

Makes about 1½ cups

8 oz. pkg. cream cheese, at room temperature
6½ oz. can crabmeat
2 Tbsp. green onion, chopped
1 Tbsp. milk
dash cayenne pepper
¼ tsp. salt
⅓ cup toasted sliced almonds

1. Combine all ingredients except almonds.
2. Spoon into ovenproof dish. Sprinkle with almonds.
3. Bake at 375°F for 15 minutes.
4. Serve on crackers.

DEVILED EGGS

Makes 24 egg halves

1 dozen hard-cooked eggs
1 small onion, grated
2 Tbsp. pickle relish
½ tsp. garlic powder
1 tsp. prepared yellow mustard
1 tsp. vinegar
salt and pepper to taste
mayonnaise
paprika

1. Slice eggs in half and remove yolks.
2. In large bowl, mash yolks. Add onion, relish, garlic powder, mustard, vinegar, salt, and pepper.
3. Add enough mayonnaise to make mixture creamy but not runny, and mix well.
4. Spoon mixture back into egg-white cups.
5. Sprinkle with paprika and chill.

GUACAMOLE

Makes about 1½ cups

2 large ripe avocados
1 tomato, chopped
1 small jalapeño pepper, finely chopped
1 Tbsp. mayonnaise
1 Tbsp. chopped onion
½ tsp. garlic salt
½ tsp. chili powder
1 Tbsp. lemon juice

1. Peel and mash avocados with a fork.
2. Add remaining ingredients and mix well.

BOILED PEANUTS

Snacking on boiled peanuts is a Deep South tradition. Some people love them, and some think they taste like unseasoned peas!

1 lb. fresh, raw peanuts in shells
1 gallon water (more or less)
10 oz. salt

1. Wash unshelled raw peanuts in cool water. Place the peanuts in a large cooking pot and cover with water. Stir in the salt. Soak peanuts in the salted water for 2 hours. It may be necessary to add more water to keep the peanuts covered, since the peanuts will absorb water as they soak.
2. Cover the pan and bring to a boil. Boil covered for about 1 hour or until peanuts are tender. Allow to stand in the hot water for about 30 minutes. Drain.
3. Serve in the shell, chilled or at room temperature.

PECAN DIP

Makes 2½ cups

8 oz. pkg. cream cheese, softened
¼ cup green pepper, finely diced
¼ cup onion, finely diced
½ tsp. garlic salt
¼ tsp. black pepper
1 cup sour cream
1 Tbsp. butter
½ cup pecans, coarsely chopped
½ tsp. salt
wheat crackers

1. Combine cream cheese, green pepper, onion, garlic salt, pepper, and sour cream. Mix well and put in a serving bowl.
2. Melt butter in a skillet; add pecans and salt. Toast over medium heat for about 5 minutes, stirring constantly. Spoon over cheese mixture.
3. Serve at room temperature with crackers.

TOMATILLO GUACAMOLE

Makes about 2½ cups

1 medium-ripe avocado
11 oz. can tomatillos, drained
1 cup chopped onion, divided
2 Tbsp. fresh cilantro
1½ tsp. serrano chile, seeded and chopped
2 Tbsp. fresh lime juice
¼ tsp. salt
¼ tsp. pepper

1. Peel and halve the avocado.
2. Place the avocado, tomatillos, half the onion, and the cilantro in a blender and process until smooth.
3. Spoon the mixture into a bowl and stir in remaining ingredients.
4. Cover and chill for at least an hour.

MEXICAN FUDGE

Makes about 18 squares

8 oz. Monterey Jack cheese, shredded
4 oz. can chopped green chiles
8 oz. cheddar cheese, shredded
1 can evaporated milk
4 eggs

1. Spread the Monterey Jack cheese on the bottom of a greased glass casserole.
2. Spread chopped chiles over the cheese.
3. Spread cheddar cheese over the chiles.
4. Mix milk and eggs together and beat well. Pour over the cheese and chili mixture.
5. Bake at 350°F for about 40 minutes.
6. Cut into 2-inch squares and serve warm with salsa.

HOT PEPPER PECANS

Makes 1 pound pecans

1 lb. pecan halves
½ cup melted butter or margarine
4 Tbsp. light soy sauce
1 tsp. Beau Monde seasoning
6 dashes pepper sauce

1. Mix pecans and butter. Place on cookie sheet.
2. Bake at 300°F for 30 minutes or until brown, stirring several times.
3. Mix soy sauce, Beau Monde, and pepper sauce. Pour over pecans and stir thoroughly.
4. Cool and store in container with tight lid.

MARINATED SHRIMP

Makes 2 lb. shrimp

2 large red onions, thinly sliced
2 lb. cooked shrimp
¼ cup vegetable oil
¾ cup white vinegar
2 tsp. hot sauce
2 tsp. celery seed
1 bottle capers with juice
2 bay leaves
½ tsp. salt

1. In large serving dish, alternate layers of onions and shrimp.
2. Mix together oil, vinegar, hot sauce, celery seed, capers, bay leaves, and salt. Pour over onions and shrimp.
3. Refrigerate for 24 hours before serving. Serve onions and shrimp in their marinade.

STUFFED MUSHROOMS

Makes 6–8 servings

1 lb. fresh mushrooms
1 cup bread crumbs
1 Tbsp. grated Parmesan cheese
1 Tbsp. chopped onion
1 small clove garlic, chopped
¼ tsp. black pepper
½ tsp. salt
2 Tbsp. vegetable oil
1 Tbsp. parsley, chopped

1. Wipe the mushrooms clean with a damp cloth and remove stems.
2. Chop stems and mix with the remaining ingredients.
3. Stuff mushroom caps and place on baking sheet.
4. Bake at 350°F for 20 minutes.

<< Stuffed Mushrooms

SPICY OYSTER CRACKERS

Makes about 2 cups crackers

16 oz. pkg. oyster crackers
¾ cup vegetable oil
1 pkg. dry ranch dressing mix
¼ tsp. lemon pepper
1 tsp. dried dillweed
¼ tsp. garlic powder

1. Mix well; then spread on an ungreased cookie sheet.
2. Bake at 350°F for 25 minutes.

PEPPER ROLLS

Makes about 2 dozen rolls

6 oz. cream cheese at room temperature
6 oz. cheddar cheese, grated
2 Tbsp. chopped black olives
3 Tbsp. chopped green chiles
1 Tbsp. grated onion
9 dashes hot sauce
2 tubes crescent rolls

1. Combine first 6 ingredients.
2. Separate crescent rolls and shape into eight rectangles (pinch two triangles together to form each rectangle). Flatten slightly with a rolling pin.
3. Spread $\frac{1}{8}$ of the cheese mixture on each rectangle. Roll up jelly roll–style and slice into ½-inch slices.
4. Place on slightly greased cookie sheet.
5. Bake for 20 minutes at 350°F.

PICO DE GALLO

Makes about 2 cups

5 medium tomatoes, chopped
2 onions, chopped
¼ cup fresh cilantro leaves, chopped
2 jalapeño peppers, seeded and chopped
juice of 2 limes
salt to taste
2 avocados, diced, *optional*

Combine all ingredients and chill.

SALSA

Makes 2 cups

---

16 oz. can tomatoes
1 clove garlic
1 small onion
2 jalapeño peppers, fresh or canned
1 Tbsp. vinegar

1. Chop tomatoes, garlic, onion, and peppers.
2. Put in a medium saucepan, along with the vinegar, and simmer over low heat for about 20 minutes until the flavors blend.
3. Bring to room temperature before serving.

TEXAS CAVIAR

Makes about 3 cups

---

2 cans black-eyed peas
½ cup salad oil
¼ cup wine vinegar
½ cup thinly sliced onions
1 clove garlic (or more)
½ tsp. salt
black pepper to taste

1. Drain peas well and place in bowl.
2. Blend oil and vinegar with remaining ingredients and add to peas.
3. Chill for one day. Remove garlic. Drain to serve.

TORTILLA ROLLS

Makes about 3 dozen servings

8 oz. pkg. cream cheese, softened
2½ oz. can chopped black olives
½ cup chopped green onions
1½ cups grated Monterey Jack cheese
½ cup sour cream
1 pkg. large tortillas

1. Mix all ingredients together except tortillas.
2. Spread on tortillas. Roll up each tortilla, jelly-roll fashion, wrap in plastic, and refrigerate overnight.
3. Slice into ½-inch slices and serve with salsa.

CORN DOGS

Makes 10 servings

Since we both have grandchildren, it seemed fitting to include a few "just for kids" snacks.

10 hot dogs
piecrust dough for 2 pies (see page 248)
¼ cup cornmeal
½ tsp. chili powder
⅛ tsp. cayenne pepper
10 wooden craft sticks

1. Prepare the piecrust recipe adding cornmeal, chili powder, and pepper.
2. Roll the crust out as for a pie. Cut into ten rectangles and wrap each around a hot dog, pressing seams, top and bottom, to make a smooth crust.
3. Insert a craft stick into one end of each hot dog. Bake on a lightly greased baking sheet at 350°F for about 20 minutes, or until lightly browned.

POPCORN BALLS

Makes about 2 dozen balls

1 stick butter
1 stick margarine
2 cups sugar
½ cup white corn syrup
1 tsp. salt
½ tsp. baking soda
1 tsp. vanilla
6 quarts popped corn (1 cup popcorn kernels equals 6 quarts popped)

1. Melt the butter and margarine in saucepan.
2. Add sugar, corn syrup, and salt.
3. Cook and stir until the mixture boils. Boil for 5 minutes.
4. Stir in the baking soda and vanilla.
5. Remove from heat and pour over the popped corn. Mix well.
6. Shape into balls.

GINA'S TRASH

Gina is our sister, and she often makes this wonderful snack. "Gina's Trash" is just what we've all come to call it!

1 stick margarine
1½ cups bacon drippings
2 Tbsp. onion powder
2 Tbsp. garlic powder
2 Tbsp. chili powder
2 Tbsp. Cajun seasoning
2 Tbsp. Worcestershire sauce
1 box Corn Chex cereal
1 box Rice Chex cereal
1 box Wheat Chex cereal
1 box Cheerios
1 small bag mini pretzels
1 can mixed nuts
1½ cups pecan halves

1. Melt the margarine and drippings. Add seasonings and Worcestershire sauce and stir well.
2. Mix together cereals, pretzels, nuts, and pecans.
3. In a large baking pan, place a layer of the cereal mixture. Sprinkle with a large spoonful of the seasonings and mix well. Add a second layer of cereal mixture and a second portion of seasonings. Repeat until all cereals, pretzels, nuts, and seasonings are used. Mix well, coating cereal with seasonings.
4. Bake at 250°F for 2–3 hours. Stir well every 30 minutes.
5. Let cool completely. Store in cookie tins.

Salads

AMBROSIA

Makes 6–8 servings

Southern holiday dinners are simply not complete without fruit salad. Ambrosia is just about everybody's favorite.

3 oranges
1 can sliced peaches
1 bottle maraschino cherries and juice
1 can crushed pineapple with juice
1½ cups flaked coconut
1 cup orange juice
½ cup peach nectar
¼ cup sugar

1. Peel oranges and remove seeds. Cut slices into small pieces. Remove as much of the white pulp from slices as you can. Place into a large mixing bowl. Set aside.
2. Remove peaches from can and cut into small pieces. Add peaches and juice to the oranges.
3. Remove cherries from jar and cut into slices. Add cherries and juice to mixture.
4. Add remaining ingredients. Mix well. Chill in refrigerator.

BARBECUED CHICKEN SALAD

Makes 4 servings

1 Tbsp. cider vinegar
1 Tbsp. sugar
2 tsp. Worcestershire sauce
¼ tsp. dry mustard
¼ tsp. hot pepper sauce
¼ tsp. black pepper
2 slices bacon
1 small onion, chopped
2 cloves garlic, minced
1 lb. chicken breast tenders, cut in ½-inch wide strips
red and green leaf lettuce
1 yellow bell pepper, cored, seeded, and cut into thin strips
1 red bell pepper, cored, seeded, and cut into thin strips
1 cup cooked or canned corn kernels, drained
2 green onions, minced (including green tops)

1. In a small bowl, combine vinegar, sugar, Worcestershire sauce, mustard, pepper sauce, and pepper. Set aside.
2. In a large skillet, cook the bacon until crisp. Drain, crumble, and set aside.
3. Drain all but 1 Tbsp. drippings from the skillet and place skillet over medium heat. Sauté onion and garlic in drippings for about 2 minutes or until softened.
4. Add the chicken and cook for about 4 minutes or until almost cooked through, stirring often.
5. Add reserved vinegar mixture to skillet, cook 1 minute longer, and then remove from heat.
6. To serve, line four salad plates with lettuce, divide bell peppers and corn among plates, top with warm chicken mixture, and garnish with crumbled bacon and green onions. Serve immediately.

RAW BEET SALAD

Makes 4 servings

3 medium-sized beets
2 stalks celery
⅓ cup chopped onion
1 grated carrot

1. Wash, peel, and coarsely chop the beets.
2. Chop the celery and onion.
3. Mix all ingredients with dressing below.

Dressing:
3 Tbsp. chopped chives
1 clove garlic
1 Tbsp. lemon juice
1 Tbsp. tarragon vinegar
½ cup chopped parsley
½ cup sour cream
½ cup mayonnaise
salt and pepper to taste

1. Combine all dressing ingredients in blender. Blend for 1 minute.
2. Chill.

MARINATED VEGETABLES

Makes 8–10 servings

9 cups assorted vegetables,
such as:
    red or green pepper strips
    carrot or celery sticks
    red onion wedges
    cauliflower
    broccoli
    fresh or frozen green beans
    fresh or frozen peas
    frozen or canned artichoke
        hearts

3 cloves garlic, minced
½ cup vegetable oil
½ cup cider vinegar
½ cup water
1 tsp. salt
1 tsp. dried oregano or Italian
    seasoning
½ tsp. black pepper
1 cup pitted ripe olives, *optional*

1. In a large pot, combine all ingredients except olives with enough lightly salted water to just cover vegetables. Bring to a boil. Reduce heat, cover, and simmer for 5 minutes or until vegetables are crisp-tender. Cool slightly.
2. Add olives. Transfer to a bowl or storage container.
3. Cover and chill for 6 hours or overnight.

BLACK-EYED PEA SALAD

Makes 6–8 servings

2 cups cooked black-eyed peas
2 large tomatoes, diced
1 cup whole-kernel corn
½ cup finely chopped green
    pepper
2 large green onions with tops,
    finely sliced
½ tsp. hot sauce

Dressing:
⅓ cup vegetable oil
2 Tbsp. vinegar
2 Tbsp. lemon juice
1 tsp. dried basil leaves, or
1 Tbsp. chopped fresh basil
    leaves
1 Tbsp. Dijon mustard
½ tsp. black pepper

1. Mix black-eyed peas, tomatoes, corn, pepper, onion, and hot sauce.
2. Combine dressing ingredients and pour over pea mixture.
3. Chill for at least 2 hours.

BROCCOLI AND GREEN OLIVE SALAD

Makes 6 servings

1 bunch fresh broccoli
1 small jar stuffed green olives
3 hard-cooked eggs
green onions and tops, chopped
¼–½ cup mayonnaise

1. Wash broccoli thoroughly and drain. Pinch flowerettes into small pieces. Peel the stalks and cut them into tiny cubes.
2. Slice each olive into about three slices and add to the broccoli.
3. Peel the hard-cooked eggs, mash fine with a fork, and add to broccoli mixture along with chopped green onions.
4. Add mayonnaise a spoonful at a time, tossing well after each addition. You do not need to add salt because the olives are salty enough.

Note:
   Add just enough mayonnaise to make the salad stick together. You do not want it to be runny.

CRANBERRY SALAD

Makes 6–8 servings

This very pretty salad looks quite festive on the table at holiday dinners.

2 cups fresh cranberries
½ cup sugar
1 small pkg. lemon gelatin
1 cup celery, finely chopped
1 cup pecans
1 apple, cored
1 orange, peeled
1 small can crushed pineapple

1. Finely chop (or grind) cranberries and then add sugar. Let stand for at least 3 hours.
2. Prepare gelatin using half the recommended amount of water.
3. Finely chop the pecans.
4. Chop apple and orange pulp. When gelatin begins to thicken, add cranberries and other ingredients.
5. Mix well and chill until completely set.

OVERNIGHT SLAW

Makes 10–12 servings

1 large head cabbage, shredded
1 green pepper, sliced thin, *optional*
1 onion, sliced in thin rings
1 cup apple cider vinegar
1 tsp. salt
2 Tbsp. prepared mustard
1½ tsp. celery seed
1 Tbsp. sugar
1 cup vegetable oil
½ cup sugar

1. Combine cabbage, pepper, and onion. Set aside.
2. In a saucepan, mix together vinegar, salt, mustard, celery seed, and 1 Tbsp. sugar. Bring to a boil.
3. Remove from heat and add oil. Bring to boil again.
4. Add ½ cup sugar, stirring well to blend. Allow to reach room temperature.
5. Pour over vegetable mixture, cover tightly, and refrigerate overnight.

CUCUMBERS IN SOUR CREAM

Makes 4–6 servings

2 medium-sized cucumbers
1 tsp. salt
½ cup sour cream
2 Tbsp. vinegar
1 Tbsp. minced green onion
½ tsp. sugar
1 tsp. dill
dash of hot sauce

1. Slice cucumbers and sprinkle with salt. Chill for at least 30 minutes. Press out any excess water with towel.
2. Combine remaining ingredients and add to cucumbers. Chill for half an hour.
3. Sprinkle with parsley or paprika.

FIVE CUP SALAD

Makes 8–10 servings

1 cup pineapple chunks, drained
1 cup miniature marshmallows
1 cup mandarin oranges, drained
1 cup chopped pecans
1 cup sour cream (low-fat works well)

Mix and chill.

CRUNCHY PEA SALAD

Makes 6 servings

6 slices bacon
1 clove garlic
2 cups green peas, well drained
½ cup chopped red onion
½ cup chopped celery
½ cup sharp cheddar cheese, cut into small pieces
3 hard-cooked eggs, chopped
1 tsp. seasoned salt
½ cup mayonnaise

1. Fry the bacon until crisp. Drain, crumble, and set aside.
2. Rub a mixing bowl lightly with garlic.
3. Mix the peas, onion, celery, cheese, eggs, bacon, and seasoned salt.
Let stand at room temperature for 1 hour.
4. Mix with just enough mayonnaise to bind the ingredients together.
5. Chill for at least 1 hour before serving.

POTATO SALAD

Makes 8 servings

3 eggs
3 medium-sized potatoes
1 stalk celery, chopped fine
3 Tbsp. finely chopped dill pickles
1 tsp. prepared mustard
4–5 Tbsp. mayonnaise
½ tsp. salt
¼ tsp. black pepper
parsley, chopped
paprika

1. Boil eggs. Peel and set aside.
2. Peel and cube potatoes. Boil potatoes until tender, drain, and set aside.
3. Put two of the eggs in a small bowl and mash well with a fork.
4. Combine the potatoes, mashed eggs, celery, pickles, mustard, mayonnaise, salt, and pepper. Mix well. Place in serving dish.
5. Slice the remaining egg lengthwise into four pieces. Arrange egg wedges over top of salad. Sprinkle with parsley and paprika and serve.

GOLDEN RICE SALAD

Makes 6 servings

1½ cups dry rice
3 cups chicken broth
¼ cup salad oil
2 Tbsp. vinegar
2 Tbsp. prepared mustard
1½ tsp. salt
¼ tsp. black pepper
1 cup chopped ripe olives

2 eggs, hard-cooked
1½ cups celery, sliced
¼ cup chopped dill pickles
¼ cup pimiento
1 small onion, diced
½ cup mayonnaise
lettuce leaves

1. Cook rice in chicken broth.
2. Blend together salad oil, vinegar, mustard, salt, and pepper and pour over the hot rice. Toss and set aside to cool.
3. Add olives, one diced egg, celery, dill pickles, pimiento, onion, and mayonnaise. Mix well. Chill thoroughly.
4. Serve on lettuce leaves and garnish with slices of remaining hard-cooked egg.

MACARONI SALAD

Makes 6–8 servings

½ cup mayonnaise
½ cup Italian salad dressing
½ cup brown mustard
½ cup celery, chopped
½ cup green pepper, chopped
4 green onions (tops included), chopped
1 lb. dry macaroni, cooked and drained

½ cup green peas, cooked and drained
4 oz. can black olives, chopped
2 oz. jar pimientos
¼ cup Parmesan cheese, grated
½ tsp. salt
½ tsp. seasoned salt
½ tsp. black pepper
dash hot sauce

1. Blend together mayonnaise, Italian dressing, and brown mustard. Set aside.
2. Combine the remaining ingredients and mix with dressing. Chill.

ORANGE SPINACH SALAD

Makes 8 servings

1 bunch raw spinach
¼ lb. mushrooms, sliced
3 oz. can water chestnuts, drained and sliced
4 oz. can mandarin orange slices, drained
2 eggs, hard-cooked and chopped
2 slices bacon, cooked, drained, and crumbled

Dressing:
¼ cup vegetable oil
2 Tbsp. vinegar
2 Tbsp. orange juice
1 scant tsp. dry mustard
¼ tsp. salt
1 tsp. soy sauce
hot sauce to taste

1. Clean and dry the spinach and break into pieces.
2. In a bowl, mix together the spinach, mushrooms, water chestnuts, orange slices, eggs, and bacon.
3. Combine the ingredients for the dressing. Mix the dressing with the salad. Refrigerate for about one hour before serving.

WILTED SPINACH SALAD

Makes 8 servings

8 cups fresh spinach
4 slices bacon, cut into small pieces
½ cup onion, chopped
2 green onions, chopped
3 Tbsp. vinegar
3 Tbsp. ketchup
1 Tbsp. sugar
2 hard-cooked eggs

1. Tear spinach leaves into bite-sized pieces and place in a mixing bowl.
2. In skillet cook bacon pieces over medium heat until crisp. Do not drain.
3. Add the chopped onions, vinegar, ketchup, and sugar. Cook, and stir until the mixture is bubbly and heated through. Remove from heat.
4. Add spinach to skillet, tossing until greens are slightly wilted and well coated. Turn back into the bowl, garnish with sliced eggs, and serve at once.

WINTER VEGETABLE SALAD

Makes 8–10 servings

1 large bunch broccoli
1 head cauliflower
3 carrots
10 oz. pkg. frozen green peas
½ cup brown mustard
½ cup mayonnaise
1½ tsp. celery seed
1½ tsp. dried tarragon, crumbled, or 1 Tbsp. fresh tarragon
½ cup Italian parsley
salt and pepper to taste

1. Trim broccoli and cauliflower and separate into florets.
2. Peel carrots and slice into ¼-inch rounds.
3. Bring a large pot of salted water to a boil. Drop broccoli into boiling water. Let water return to a boil and cook for 1 minute. Remove broccoli from water with slotted spoon or skimmer and allow to cool.
4. Drop cauliflower into same boiling water. Let water return to a boil and cook for 2 minutes. Remove cauliflower and cool.
5. Repeat the blanching process with the carrots and the peas in the same pot of water, boiling each for 1 minute. Remove and cool.
6. Drain all vegetables thoroughly and combine in a large mixing bowl.
7. Mix remaining ingredients together in a small bowl and pour over vegetables. Toss gently but thoroughly and chill before serving.

SHRIMP SALAD

Makes 6 servings

1 cup mayonnaise
1 Tbsp. Worcestershire sauce
1 tsp. shrimp base
2 tsp. hot sauce
1 tsp. hot mustard
1½ lb. shrimp, cooked and deveined
¾ cup celery, chopped
½ cup green onion, chopped
1 tsp. black pepper
1 tsp. seasoned salt
greens

1. Combine mayonnaise, Worcestershire sauce, shrimp base, hot sauce, and mustard.
2. Add shrimp, celery, onion, pepper, and salt. Chill and serve on a bed of greens.

Note:
  Look for shrimp base in the spice section of your grocery store.

STRAWBERRY PRETZEL SALAD

Makes 6–8 servings

¾ cup margarine at room temperature
3 Tbsp. brown sugar
2½ cups crushed pretzels
1 large box strawberry gelatin
2 cups boiling water
3 cups strawberries, sliced
8 oz. pkg. cream cheese at room temperature
1 cup powdered sugar
1 small box whipped topping

1. Cream margarine and brown sugar.
2. Mix in crushed pretzels.
3. Pat into 13″ x 9″ baking pan.
4. Bake at 350°F for about 10 minutes. Cool.
5. Dissolve gelatin in boiling water and add strawberries. Chill until almost set.
6. Meanwhile, mix cream cheese with powdered sugar. Fold in whipped topping. Spread over the cooled crust.
7. Pour on the strawberry mixture. Chill and cut into squares when set.

Soups

APPLE CIDER SOUP

Makes 4 servings

2 tart cooking apples
¼ cup rice, uncooked
1 cup apple cider
½ cup raisins
¼ cup water
2 Tbsp. applejack, or schnapps
½ tsp. ground cinnamon
¼ tsp. nutmeg
1 Tbsp. brown sugar

1. Peel, core, and chop the apples.
2. Combine all ingredients in a large saucepan. Stir well and bring to a boil.
3. Cover and simmer for 30 minutes, stirring occasionally.
4. Serve hot with a dollop of topping.

Topping
½ cup sour cream
1 tsp. sugar
¼ tsp. vanilla

Mix well and use to top apple cider soup.

BAKED POTATO SOUP

Makes 8–10 servings

3 large potatoes
½ cup celery, chopped
¾ cup onion, chopped
½ cup green onions, chopped
2 cloves garlic, minced
½ cup carrot, grated
1 tsp. seasoned salt
1 tsp. black pepper
6 slices bacon
2 Tbsp. olive oil
2 cups chicken broth
2⅔ cups half-and-half
12 oz. Swiss cheese, grated
2 Tbsp. butter
⅓ cup flour

1. Bake the potatoes, peel, and cut into ½-inch cubes. Set aside.
2. Combine celery, onion, green onions, garlic, and carrot.
3. Add salt and pepper. Set aside.
4. Dice the bacon and cook over medium high heat in a Dutch oven until brown. Reduce heat to medium low and add oil.
5. When hot, add vegetable mixture and sauté until vegetables are soft.
6. Add potato cubes and cook until they start to brown.
7. Add broth and half-and-half and cook over medium heat, stirring constantly for 5 minutes.
8. Fold in cheese, stirring until thoroughly blended.
9. Heat margarine in a saucepan over low heat. Whisk in flour and cook for 5 minutes to make a roux. Add the roux to the soup and stir until thoroughly blended.
10. Reduce heat and simmer, stirring occasionally for 30 minutes, until soup is heated through.

BEEF STEW

Makes 8 servings

2 medium-sized potatoes
¼ cup vegetable oil
1 lb. boneless stewing meat
3 Tbsp. self-rising flour
1 onion, chopped
½ cup bell pepper, chopped
½ cup celery, chopped
1 clove garlic, minced
¼ cup parsley flakes
1 can tomatoes with chiles,
    mashed

1 can tomato sauce
1 can beef broth
1 can water
5–6 carrots, cubed
salt to taste
½ tsp. lemon pepper
red pepper to taste
½ tsp. beef-flavor seasoning
1 small can green peas, *optional*

1. Peel and cut up potatoes. Cover with tap water and set aside.
2. Heat oil in a large heavy pot.
3. Rinse and cut meat into small pieces. Drop meat into hot oil and brown on all sides until very dark.
4. Add flour and stir vigorously.
5. Add onion, bell pepper, celery, garlic, and parsley. Stir well.
6. Add tomatoes, tomato sauce, beef broth, and one broth can of water. Simmer over medium heat for 1 hour.
7. Add drained potatoes and carrots.
8. Add salt, lemon pepper, red pepper, and beef flavoring. Cook for about 25 minutes or until potatoes and carrots are tender.
9. Add peas right before turning the burner off or reducing heat to warm.
10. Serve over rice.

My husband likes this stew served over cheese grits, with homemade buttermilk biscuits alongside.

Note:
   You may substitute leftover roast beef for the stewing meat.

BLACK BEAN SOUP

Makes 8 servings

12 oz. dried black beans
8 cups chicken broth
ham bone with about ½ lb. ham attached
2 tsp. olive oil
1 onion, chopped
1 green pepper, chopped
1 cup celery, chopped
2 cloves garlic, minced
2 tsp. dried oregano
1 tsp. dried thyme
2 bay leaves
½ tsp. cayenne pepper
3 Tbsp. fresh lime juice
chopped green onion or cilantro for garnish
salt and pepper to taste

1. Rinse and sort through beans, discarding any stones. Place beans in a large stockpot. Cover with water and refrigerate while soaking overnight.
2. Drain beans and return to stockpot.
3. Add chicken broth and ham bone and bring to a boil.
4. Heat olive oil over medium heat in a skillet. Add onion, green pepper, celery, and garlic. Sauté until tender, approximately 5 minutes. Add to stockpot.
5. Stir oregano, thyme, bay leaves, and cayenne pepper into stockpot.
6. Cover stockpot and reduce heat to low. Simmer for 3–4 hours.
7. Transfer ⅔ of the soup to a blender and puree. Transfer back to stockpot and stir into remaining beans.
8. Just before serving, add lime juice and garnish with green onion or cilantro if desired. Add salt and pepper to taste.

HAMBURGER SOUP

Makes 8 servings

1 lb. lean ground beef
1 onion, chopped
2 cloves garlic, minced
2 cans whole or stewed tomatoes
1 tsp. salt
1 tsp. black pepper
2½ tsp. cumin
3 quarts chicken broth
2 cans cream-style corn
½ cup cornstarch
1 cup cool water
9 oz. pkg. corn tortillas
2 cups shredded American cheese, divided
vegetable oil

1. In a large Dutch oven, brown ground beef with chopped onion and garlic. Drain well.
2. Crush the tomatoes and add when meat is done.
3. Add salt, pepper, and cumin, and stir well.
4. Add broth and corn, and bring to a boil. Let simmer for about 15 minutes.
5. In a small bowl, dissolve cornstarch in cool water, mixing well. Add to the soup mixture, stirring well until dissolved and soup is thickened.
6. Cut the tortillas into 1" x 3" strips. Add half of strips and half of cheese to soup.
7. Allow soup to return to a simmer, but do not allow to boil.
8. Heat oil in skillet and add remaining tortilla strips. Fry until strips are crisp. Drain strips on paper towels.
9. Garnish soup in bowls with crisp tortilla strips and remaining grated cheese.

CHEESY HAMBURGER SOUP

Makes 8 servings

½ lb. ground beef
¾ cup chopped onion
1 tsp. dried basil
1 tsp. dried parsley flakes
3 cups chicken broth
4 cups potatoes, diced
4 Tbsp. butter or margarine, divided
¼ cup all-purpose flour
2 cups (8 oz.) American cheese, cubed
1½ cups milk
½ tsp. salt
½ tsp. pepper
¼ cup sour cream

1. In a large saucepan, sauté ground beef, onion, basil, and parsley for about 10 minutes, or until meat is cooked through and browned.
2. Add broth and diced potatoes. Reduce heat and simmer for 10–12 minutes or until potatoes are tender.
3. In a small skillet, melt butter and stir in the flour. Cook for about 5 minutes or until bubbly, and add to the soup. Cook for about 5 minutes, stirring often.
4. Reduce heat to low and add cheese, milk, salt, and pepper. Cook and stir until the cheese melts.
5. Remove from heat and blend in the sour cream just before serving.

CHEESE BROCCOLI SOUP

Makes 4 servings

1½ lb. fresh broccoli, pared and chopped
1 pint half-and-half
2 cups water
1 lb. American cheese, grated or cubed
¾ tsp. salt
½ tsp. pepper
½ cup cornstarch
1 cup cold water

1. Steam broccoli until tender.
2. Place half-and-half and water in the top of a double boiler.
3. Add cheese, salt, and pepper. Heat, stirring frequently, until all the cheese is melted.
4. Add steamed broccoli.
5. Combine cornstarch and water in a small bowl. Stir into cheese mixture in the top of the double boiler and continue to heat over simmering water until soup thickens.

CHICKEN GUMBO

Makes 6–8 servings

This recipe comes from our mother, Jane McQueen. The recipe calls for gumbo file, the Creole name for powdered sassafras, which is used as a thickener for stews and soups.

1 chicken, cut up
salt
4 Tbsp. vegetable oil
4 Tbsp. self-rising flour
1 onion, chopped
2–3 pods of okra, cut up
1 tsp. gumbo file
salt and pepper to taste
1 can chicken broth or chicken gravy, *optional*

1. Cover chicken with lightly salted water in a pot and boil on medium heat for approximately 45 minutes. When cooked through, you may debone the chicken or leave it in pieces. Reserve the broth.
2. In a separate pan, combine the oil and flour until smooth. Cook roux over medium heat until very brown.
3. Stir in onions and okra. Simmer over low heat for about 10 minutes. Add the roux to the chicken and broth.
4. Continue cooking over medium heat until thoroughly blended, about 10–15 minutes. Turn heat down to simmer, and add the gumbo file, salt, and pepper. Stir well.
5. Let gumbo rest 2–3 minutes, and then serve over rice. If the texture is too thick, add one can chicken broth. If it is too thin, add one can chicken gravy.

***Note**:*

I usually add one can of oysters about 15 minutes before I discontinue cooking. I also sprinkle a little chopped parsley over the gumbo before serving it.

SPICY CHICKEN SOUP

Makes 8 servings

1 whole chicken, skinned and cut in pieces
3 10½ oz. cans condensed chicken broth
2 10 oz. cans diced tomatoes with green chiles
16 oz. pkg. frozen whole-kernel corn
1 large onion, chopped
4 cloves garlic, minced
1 tsp. dried oregano

1. Combine all ingredients in stockpot. Bring to boil over medium high heat.
2. Cover, reduce heat, and simmer for 2 hours, stirring occasionally.
3. Remove chicken and cool. Debone chicken and cut meat into bite-sized pieces. Return the meat to the pot.
4. Simmer for 15 minutes, stirring occasionally.

QUICK CORN, SAUSAGE, AND HAM CHOWDER

Makes 8 servings

2 cups frozen hash brown potatoes
1 Tbsp. margarine
1 cup cooked ham, diced
1 can whole-kernel corn
2 cups milk
1 cup onion, chopped
1 cup smoked sausage, diced
1 can cream-style corn
1 can cream of mushroom soup
salt and pepper to taste

1. Combine all ingredients in large pot. Cook on low for 35 minutes, stirring occasionally.
2. Serve with jalapeño cornbread.

CRAWFISH BISQUE

Makes 6–8 servings

¼ lb. (1 stick) margarine
1 cup flour
½ cup onion, chopped
½ cup green bell pepper, chopped
½ cup celery, chopped
1½ Tbsp. Creole seasoning
2 Tbsp. crushed beef bouillon cubes
6 cups boiling water
2 lb. crawfish tail meat
½ Tbsp. bottled browning sauce (such as Kitchen Bouquet)
salt to taste

1. In a large stockpot, melt margarine over medium heat. Add flour to make a roux and cook, stirring constantly until roux turns a dark brown.
2. Mix in onion, bell pepper, and celery.
3. Add seasoning and crushed bouillon cubes.
4. Add boiling water and stir over medium-high heat until thickened.
5. Add crawfish, browning sauce, and salt. Heat until warmed through. Serve over rice.

CHILI

Makes 8 servings

1 large onion, chopped
2 cloves garlic, minced
2 Tbsp. vegetable oil
2 lb. lean, coarsely ground beef
1 large can tomatoes
2 small cans tomato sauce
2 tsp. cumin
2 tsp. paprika
2 cups chicken broth
4 Tbsp. chili powder
1 fresh jalapeño pepper, seeded and chopped
salt to taste
cayenne pepper to taste
shredded cheese and green onions for garnish (optional)

1. Sauté chopped onion and garlic in oil.
2. Add meat and stir continuously until meat begins to brown.
3. Stir in remaining ingredients. Cover and cook gently over medium heat for about 1½ hours. Stir occasionally. Garnish with shredded cheese and chopped green onions, if desired.

WHITE CHILI

Makes 6–8 servings

1 Tbsp. olive oil
salt and pepper to taste
2 cups boneless chicken, cubed
½ cup chopped onion
2 cloves garlic
1½ cups chicken broth
4 oz. can chopped green chiles

1 tsp. ground cumin
½ tsp. cilantro leaves
⅛ tsp. cayenne pepper
19 oz. can white kidney beans,
    undrained
2 green onions, chopped
Monterey Jack cheese

1. Heat oil in large saucepan over medium heat.
2. Very lightly salt and pepper chicken pieces.
3. Sauté onion, garlic, and chicken pieces in oil for about 5 minutes.
4. Stir in broth, green chiles, and spices. Simmer for 15 minutes.
5. Stir in beans. Simmer for about 10 minutes.
6. Garnish with chopped green onions and grated Monterey Jack cheese just before serving.

OYSTER STEW

Makes 8 servings

½ cup onion, diced
¼ cup celery, diced
½ cup green peppers, diced
2 Tbsp. butter
1 Tbsp. flour

salt and pepper to taste
1 quart oysters, chopped
4 cups half-and-half
dash of hot sauce, *optional*

1. Sauté the vegetables in butter in a heavy saucepan.
2. Stir in the flour, salt, and pepper, mixing well.
3. Add the oysters and cook for about 5 minutes.
4. Stir in the half-and-half and cook over low heat for about 10–12 minutes. Do not allow stew to boil. If you like, just before serving, add a dash of hot sauce.

ROUX

So many Southern soup recipes begin, "First you make a roux." A roux, used both to add flavor and to thicken a broth or sauce, usually consists of equal parts of flour and shortening or vegetable oil. Stir the flour into the oil, heating the mixture slowly over low heat until it becomes smooth and eventually reaches a chocolate-brown color. This can take about 30 minutes. The mixture must be stirred frequently to keep it from burning. The following roux can be made easily in the microwave oven if you want to save time.

Microwave Roux:
½ cup flour
½ cup vegetable oil

1. Place flour and oil in a large microwave-safe bowl and blend well with a whisk or spoon.
2. Microwave on high for 6–8 minutes, stopping often to stir and to turn the bowl. When the roux thickens and reaches a chocolate color, it is finished and can be added to the recipe for which it was being prepared.

SEAFOOD GUMBO

Makes 8 servings

Gumbo file both seasons and thickens stews and soups.

4 inches smoked sausage
1 chicken breast
3–4 Tbsp. vegetable oil
3–4 Tbsp. self-rising flour
2 hard-cooked eggs, mashed fine
    with a fork
1 cup onion, chopped
1 cup bell pepper, chopped
1 jalapeño pepper, chopped,
    optional
1 cup celery, chopped

½ cup parsley, chopped
3 cloves garlic, minced
1 can tomato paste
1 can stewed tomatoes
2 cans water (use stewed tomato
    can to measure)
1–2 lb. raw shrimp, peeled
1–2 cans crabmeat
2 tsp. gumbo file
salt and pepper to taste
chopped green onion tops

1. Precook sausage in a small skillet until well done. Drain off oil, cut into bite-sized pieces, and set aside.
2. Boil chicken breast until tender in just enough water to cover. Remove from broth, debone, and cut into bite-size pieces. Set aside. Save broth.
3. Make a roux with the oil and flour (browning flour in the oil).
4. Add eggs, onion, bell pepper, jalapeño pepper, celery, parsley, and garlic.
5. Add broth from the chicken, tomato paste, stewed tomatoes, and water. Bring to a medium boil and cook for approximately 45 minutes, stirring often.
6. Add raw shrimp, crabmeat, sausage, and chicken. Cook for 20 more minutes on a medium boil.
7. Add salt and pepper to taste. Add file, but do not boil after adding.
8. Garnish with chopped green onion tops.

Note:
    Add ¼ tsp. of concentrated shrimp and crab boil liquid to your gumbo while in the last cooking stage. This adds a very hot flavor. The "boil" can be found in the spice section of many grocery stores.

Option:
    Sometimes I cut up ½ cup okra and add it with the seasonings, onions, bell pepper, etc. It depends on who I'm cooking for. Some people do not like okra!

OKRA SOUP

Makes 8 servings

1 lb. cubed lean stewing meat
1 soup bone, *optional*
1 large onion, chopped
2 bay leaves
1 beef bouillon cube
2 quarts water
2 lb. fresh okra, finely diced
2 16 oz. cans tomatoes
salt and pepper to taste
1 can whole-kernel corn

1. In a large saucepan, boil the meat, soup bone, onion, bay leaves, and bouillon cube in the water for 1 hour, stirring occasionally.
2. Add the okra and cook for 30 minutes.
3. Add the tomatoes, salt, and pepper and cook for another 30 minutes.
4. Add the corn and cook for one more hour.
5. Add more water if soup becomes too thick as it cooks.

POBLANO CREAM SOUP

Makes 6 servings

1 onion, chopped
3 cloves garlic, minced
½ cup chopped green pepper
½ cup grated carrot
½ cup chopped celery
1 Tbsp. vegetable oil
1 cup poblano peppers, finely
    diced
4 Tbsp. butter or margarine
½ cup flour

1 chicken bouillon cube
½ cup hot water
2 cups half-and-half
2 cups whole milk
½ tsp. salt
½ tsp. black pepper
½ tsp. cayenne pepper
1 cup shredded Monterey Jack
    cheese

1. In a large saucepan, sauté onion, garlic, green pepper, carrot, and celery in oil over medium heat until soft, about 4 minutes.
2. Add poblano peppers and sauté for about 3 minutes. Remove vegetables from the pan and set aside.
3. In the same pan that you cooked the vegetables, make roux by melting butter and stirring in the flour until smooth.
4. In small bowl, dissolve bouillon cube in water.
5. Stir half-and-half, milk, and bouillon water into roux. Stir constantly over heat until thickened.
6. Add salt and peppers. Simmer over medium low heat for about 25 minutes, stirring frequently.
7. Add cheese and stir until melted. Taste and adjust seasonings, if necessary.

FALL VEGETABLE SOUP

Makes 8 servings

¼ cup butter
1 large onion, finely chopped
3 green onions, chopped
1 large potato, peeled and diced
1 cup carrots, sliced
2 cups butternut squash, cut into
½-inch cubes

3 cups chicken broth
2 cups light cream
½ cup white wine or apple cider,
    optional
salt and pepper to taste

1. In a large saucepan, melt butter. Add onion and green onions. Cook until soft.
2. Add potato, carrots, and squash. Cook for about 3 minutes, stirring often.
3. Add the broth. Cover and cook for about 25 minutes or until vegetables are tender.
4. Puree in blender until very smooth. Return to saucepan.
5. Stir in cream to desired consistency. Add wine. Heat slowly until very hot (do not boil).
6. Season with salt and pepper.

PUMPKIN SOUP

Makes 4–6 servings

½ cup onion, chopped
¼ cup butter
¼ tsp. ground ginger
¼ tsp. ground nutmeg
3 cups chicken broth

2 cups canned pumpkin puree
1 cup half-and-half
2 Tbsp. brandy
salt to taste
white pepper to taste

1. Sauté onion in butter until transparent. Blend in the spices and broth. Bring to a boil.
2. Stir in puree and half-and-half. Reduce the heat and cook until the soup is heated through (but not boiling), stirring occasionally.
3. Blend in brandy.
4. Add salt and pepper to taste. Serve hot.

<< Pumpkin Soup

SPINACH SOUP

Makes 4–6 servings

1 bunch fresh spinach, or 1 pkg. frozen spinach
3 Tbsp. melted butter or margarine
½ cup onion, chopped
1 tsp. lemon juice
1½ cups chicken broth
1 cup milk
1 cup half-and-half
½ tsp. black pepper
¼ tsp. nutmeg
Parmesan cheese

1. Cover spinach with lightly salted water and bring to boil. Remove from heat. Do not drain.
2. Place cooked spinach, butter, onion, lemon juice, and broth in blender container. Blend thoroughly.
3. In a large saucepan, mix the spinach mixture with milk, half-and-half, pepper, and nutmeg. Heat thoroughly but do not allow to boil.
4. Serve hot with Parmesan cheese grated on top.

PEANUT SOUP

Makes 6–8 servings

1 small onion, diced
2 ribs celery, diced
¼ lb. (1 stick) butter
3 Tbsp. flour
2 quarts chicken broth
1 pint peanut butter
½ tsp. celery salt
1 tsp. salt
1 Tbsp. lemon juice
½ cup raw peanuts, ground

1. Sauté onion and celery in the butter for 5 minutes (don't brown).
2. Add flour and mix well.
3. Blend in broth and cook for 30 minutes. Remove from heat. Strain.
4. Add peanut butter, celery salt, salt, and lemon juice. Simmer for 15 minutes.
5. Sprinkle ground peanuts on soup just before serving.

TOMATO BASIL SOUP

Makes 6–8 servings

3 Tbsp. olive oil
2 carrots, chopped
1 large onion, chopped
4 cups chicken stock
1½ tsp. fresh thyme, or ½ tsp. dried thyme
½ tsp. paprika
1 cup tomato juice
3 lb. fresh plum tomatoes
1 cup loosely packed fresh basil leaves, divided
salt and pepper to taste

1. Heat oil in large stockpot over medium heat.
2. Add carrots and onion and sauté for about 5 minutes.
3. Stir in stock, thyme, and paprika. Bring to a simmer and cook for 10 minutes, stirring constantly.
4. Add tomato juice, tomatoes, and half the basil. Return to a simmer and cook, uncovered, for about 40 minutes.
5. Remove from heat and add remaining basil.
6. In small batches, pulse soup two or three times in a blender to form a slightly chunky puree. Return puree to pot and reheat gently.
7. Season with salt and pepper.

Vegetables

COUNTRY COOKED FRESH VEGETABLES

Makes 4–6 servings

fresh vegetable of your choice
2 slices of bacon, or ½ cup cooked ham
¼ cup minced onion or green onion
salt and pepper to taste

Vegetable Options: (fresh or frozen)
    speckled butter beans
    green beans
    green lima beans
    field peas
    crowder peas

1. Rinse vegetables well, whether using fresh or frozen.
2. Fry two slices of bacon (or ham) in cooking pot.
3. Add onion and cook for 3–5 minutes.
4. Add one of the above vegetables and one cup of water. Bring to a hard boil. Cook for 15 minutes on a hard boil. Reduce heat to a slow boil and simmer for 30 more minutes.
5. Season to taste. Add water as needed for the amount of juices desired.

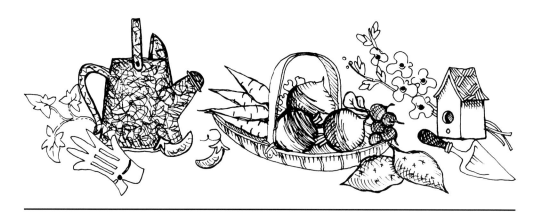

RED BEANS AND SAUSAGE

Makes 6–8 servings

1 pkg. dry red beans
1 slice bacon
½ tsp. salt
¼ tsp. black pepper
1 large onion, chopped
½ lb. smoked pork sausage, cut in bite-size pieces
½ cup green onions, chopped

1. Place beans in a colander and rinse thoroughly with hot tap water. Place beans in stockpot in enough water to cover them fully.
2. Cut bacon in four pieces and add to pot.
3. Add salt and pepper.
4. Add chopped onion and cook on medium boil for 1 hour, stirring often and adding water as needed.
5. While the beans are cooking, place the sausage into a pot on medium heat. Cover the pot with a lid. Turn the sausage often, letting it cook in its own oil for approximately 20 minutes. Drain all oil and discard.
6. Add the sausage to the beans and continue to cook on low to medium heat for another hour. Every 30 minutes test a bean with a fork to see if it is tender.
7. When the beans are nearly tender, if the bean gravy is not as thick as you would like, remove ½ cup of beans, mash them with a fork, and return them to the pot. This will add thickness to the gravy.
8. About 10 minutes before serving, add chopped green onions and turn burner off. Serve over cooked rice.

BEER BEANS

Makes 8 servings

This is a no-fuss way to cook a tasty pot of beans on a cold day. Serve with cornbread.

½ lb. ground beef
1 medium onion, chopped
1 green pepper, chopped
1 clove garlic
2 16 oz. cans ranch-style beans

1 small can whole-kernel corn
1 cup green olives
8 oz. can mushroom pieces
1 can tomatoes with chiles
16 oz. can beer

1. Brown meat with onion, green pepper, and garlic. Drain.
2. Combine remaining ingredients with meat mixture in a large saucepan (or slow cooker). Simmer for 3 or 4 hours, stirring occasionally.

SOUTHERN LIMA BEANS

Makes 6 servings

4 slices bacon
½ cup onion, chopped
2 10 oz. pkg. frozen green lima
   beans
½ tsp. salt

½ tsp. black pepper
1 tomato, chopped
½ cup grated cheddar cheese
4 Tbsp. bread crumbs

1. Cook the bacon until crisp. Drain and crumble.
2. Remove all but 1 Tbsp. bacon drippings and add onion. Sauté until tender and set aside.
3. In a buttered 2-quart casserole dish, mix the bacon, onion, beans, salt, pepper, tomato, and cheese. Sprinkle with bread crumbs and bake for 25 minutes at 350°F.

DRY WHITE LIMA BEANS

Makes 8 servings

2 cups dry white lima beans
1 strip bacon
½ cup chopped onion
salt and pepper to taste
2 chopped green onions and tops

1. Place beans in colander and rinse well under cold running water. Place beans in stockpot. Fill with water twice the height of the beans. Boil for 3 minutes.
2. Drain beans and rinse again in colander, this time with hot water. Return beans to stockpot. Fill with fresh water twice the height of the beans and bring to a boil again. Boil for 3 minutes.
3. Drain beans and rinse again in colander with hot water. Place beans in fresh water (again, twice the height of the beans) for the third time and bring to boil, this time adding the bacon strip and onions. Cook on a medium boil for about 1 hour, adding hot water as needed.
4. When the beans are tender, add salt and pepper to taste. Sprinkle with green onions and stir.
5. Serve over rice.

Notes:

1. Boiling the beans and discarding the water several times prevents them from becoming yellow or dark. They stay whiter this way.

2. Cook navy or Great Northern dry beans exactly the same way—by bringing to a boil several times in fresh water.

OLD-FASHIONED BAKED BEANS

Makes 8–10 servings

2 cups dried navy beans
13 cups water, divided
½ cup brown sugar, packed
¼ cup molasses
1 tsp. salt
6 slices bacon, fried crisp and crumbled
1 medium onion

1. Heat Dutch oven to 350°F.
2. Heat the beans and 10 cups water to boiling in the Dutch oven. Boil uncovered 2 minutes.
3. Stir in remaining ingredients except 3 cups water. Cover and bake for 4 hours, stirring occasionally.
4. Stir in remaining 3 cups water.
5. Bake uncovered for 2 hours longer, stirring occasionally, until beans are tender and of desired consistency.

BEETS WITH VINEGAR SAUCE

Makes 4 servings

2 cups beets
2 Tbsp. cornstarch
½ tsp. salt
1½ Tbsp. honey
2 Tbsp. cider vinegar
2 Tbsp. butter or margarine

1. Wash, peel, and chop the beets.
2. Boil with just enough water to cover until tender. Drain, reserving ⅓ cup of the beet juice.
3. In small saucepan mix cornstarch, salt, honey, and vinegar with reserved beet juice and stir until smooth. Cook until clear and thickened.
4. Add butter. Pour over beets.
5. Bake in a 350°F oven until heated through.

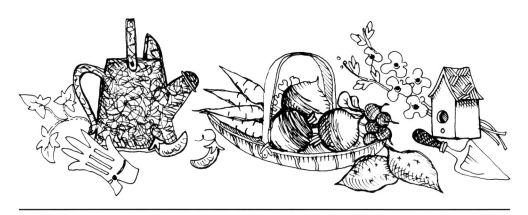

CREAMED CABBAGE

Makes 6 servings

4 cups cabbage, chopped
2 Tbsp. butter or margarine
½ cup flour
2 cups milk
salt and pepper to taste

1 cup toasted bread crumbs,
   divided
¾ cup grated sharp cheddar
   cheese, divided

1. Boil chopped cabbage in a very small amount of lightly salted water for 10 minutes or until cabbage is just tender. Drain, reserving liquid.
2. Melt butter in saucepan and stir in flour. Add milk to mixture, stirring constantly. Cook until the sauce begins to thicken. Add a little cabbage broth to thin the sauce. Season with salt and pepper.
3. Add drained cabbage, half the crumbs, and half the cheese to the sauce.
4. Place cabbage and sauce in buttered casserole dish and sprinkle with the remaining cheese and crumbs.
5. Bake in a 350°F oven for 30 minutes.

BAKED CARROTS AND MUSHROOMS

Makes 6–8 servings

2 sticks (½ lb.) margarine
⅛ cup Worcestershire sauce
1½ lb. fresh whole mushrooms
2 lb. fresh whole baby carrots

2 onions, cut into large pieces
2 cloves garlic, minced
½ tsp. salt
½ tsp. black pepper

1. Melt margarine in a baking dish in preheated 375°F oven. Remove from oven and add Worcestershire sauce. Stir well.
2. Add all other ingredients and return to oven.
3. Bake 1 hour, or until carrots and onions are tender.

DILLED CARROTS

Makes 4–6 servings

1 lb. carrots
1 cup Italian salad dressing
½ cup grated onion
2 tsp. parsley flakes
2 Tbsp. dillweed
1 tsp. salt
½ tsp. black pepper

1. Scrub, then slice carrots in ½-inch slices. Cover with lightly salted water and boil until crisp tender, about 8–10 minutes.
2. Combine remaining ingredients. Pour over carrots and marinate for 24–48 hours. Serve cold.

GLAZED CARROTS

Makes 4–6 servings

10 carrots
½ cup fresh orange juice
1½ Tbsp. butter
¼ tsp. ginger
¼ tsp. cinnamon
1½ Tbsp. light brown sugar
1½ Tbsp. granulated sugar

1. Slice carrots ¼-inch thick.
2. In a skillet, combine all ingredients. Bring the liquid to a boil and reduce heat to a simmer. Cover and cook for about 6 minutes. Uncover and continue to simmer until the carrots are crisp tender and most of the liquid has evaporated.

STUFFED CAULIFLOWER

Makes 6 servings

1 head cauliflower
1 cup lightly salted water
2 Tbsp. butter or margarine
2 Tbsp. flour
1 cup milk
½ tsp. salt
¼ tsp. black pepper
2 hard-cooked eggs, chopped
2 Tbsp. green onions, finely chopped
¼ cup buttered bread crumbs
½ cup cheddar cheese, grated

1. Place cauliflower and water in a large Dutch oven. Boil for about 10 minutes. Remove from heat and cool.
2. In a skillet, melt the butter and blend in the flour. Add milk, stirring constantly. Cook until thick and smooth.
3. Add the salt, pepper, chopped eggs, and green onions, and simmer for 5 minutes.
4. Place the cauliflower in a buttered baking dish. Carefully cut off the top of the cauliflower and set it aside. Scoop out some of the center of the cauliflower "stalk." Chop the scooped-out cauliflower and add to half the sauce (reserve the other half of sauce).
5. Fill the center with the sauce and cauliflower mixture. Replace the top. Pour the reserved sauce over the cauliflower. Sprinkle with bread crumbs and grated cheese.
6. Bake in a 350°F oven for 30 minutes.

COUNTRY FRIED CORN

Makes 4–6 servings

8–10 ears fresh corn
2 slices bacon
½ cup onion, finely chopped
¼ cup water
salt to taste
black pepper to taste

1. Remove shucks and silk from corn. Rinse and blot dry with paper towels. Set aside.
2. Fry bacon in a 2–3-quart stockpot. Remove bacon and add chopped onion to the bacon drippings. Simmer on low to medium heat for 5 minutes. Break each slice of bacon into 3 pieces and stir into the onions. Remove stockpot from heat and set aside.
3. Shave the corn off the cob all the way around with a very sharp knife. Shave a second time all the way around. Take a duller knife and scrape corn and juices into bowl. Repeat this step with each ear of corn. When you have finished scraping the corn, discard the cobs. Corn should be of a very stiff but soupy consistency. Pour into stockpot with bacon and onions and place on a medium burner.
4. Add water, salt, and pepper. Stir up from the bottom of the pot frequently since the corn scorches very easily. Cook for 20–25 minutes. Turn the burner to a low simmer and continue cooking for 35 more minutes.

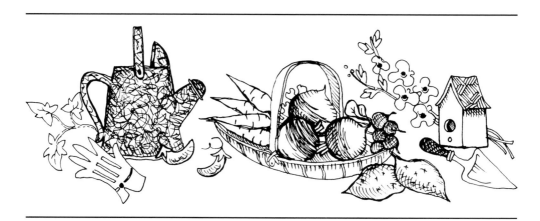

SOUTH LOUISIANA EGGPLANT

Makes 4–5 servings

1 medium eggplant
2 medium tomatoes, diced
1 clove garlic, minced
¾ cup green onions, chopped
¼ cup fresh parsley, chopped
5 Tbsp. red wine vinegar
3 Tbsp. olive oil
1 tsp. ground cumin
½ tsp. hot sauce
½ tsp. salt

1. Trim ends off the eggplant and cut in half lengthwise. Place the halves on a greased baking sheet, cut side down.
2. Bake at 375°F for 35 minutes or until tender. Cool, peel, and dice.
3. In a large bowl, mix eggplant, tomatoes, garlic, green onions, and parsley.
4. In a small bowl, stir together remaining ingredients. Pour the marinade over the vegetables and mix well.
5. Cover and let stand for several hours to blend flavors. Serve at room temperature.

BOILED FRESH GREENS

Fresh greens—turnip greens, mustard, collards, or chard—were often cooked in a salt pork-laced vinegary liquid, which Southerners called "pot likker." Once all of the greens were spooned out, the remaining juice or pot likker was eaten like a soup, usually with cornbread.

ham hock or thick-sliced bacon
diced onion
2–3 cups water
turnip greens, mustard greens, collard, or chard (or a mixture)
salt and pepper to taste

1. Boil ham hock and onion in 2–3 cups water for approximately 30 minutes. If using bacon, sauté until browned, then carefully add 2–3 cups water, being aware that the hot grease in the pan may splatter.
2. Add washed and cut-up greens. Bring to a boil and reduce heat to a low to medium boil.
3. Cook for 30–35 minutes, adding water as needed. Salt and pepper to taste.
4. If desired, cut up the meat into small pieces and mix into cooked greens.

SAUTÉED GREENS

chopped onion and garlic, according to the amount of greens used
2 Tbsp. oil
any kind of greens—turnip, mustard or collard greens, chard or
    spinach (or a mixture), cleaned and chopped
whatever herbs are growing in the garden—basil and oregano, for sure
salt and pepper to taste
cider or tarragon vinegar

1. Sauté onion and garlic in oil for about 5 minutes.
2. Quickly drop in clean, chopped greens.
3. Add chopped herbs. Stir quickly.
4. Reduce heat to low. Cook for 15–20 minutes (or longer depending on the toughness of the greens) until vegetables are barely tender.
5. Add salt and pepper.
6. Sprinkle with vinegar and serve.

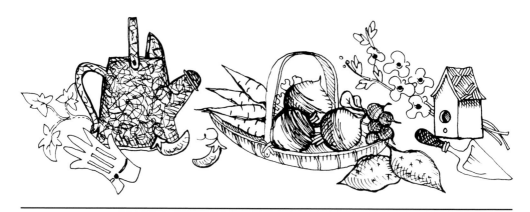

HOMINY

Makes 2 servings

"Hominy" is thought to be a derivation of an Indian word, rockahominie, *meaning parched corn. Hominy is corn treated with lye water to soften the grains and remove the hulls. Ashes from a wood fire were put into an ash hopper, and water was poured over the ashes. A crock placed beneath the hopper caught the water as it dripped through the ashes. Shelled corn was left to soak in this lye water overnight. The corn was drained, tumbled to remove the hulls, and washed thoroughly. It was then boiled several times before it was tender enough to eat. Today, hominy is available at the grocery store in cans!*

3 slices bacon, minced
¼ cup onion, chopped
1 can hominy
salt and pepper to taste

1. Fry bacon over medium heat. Remove bacon and all but about 1 tsp. of the drippings.
2. Sauté onion in bacon drippings until soft.
3. Add hominy and bacon pieces and cook for about 15 minutes.
4. Season to taste.

CHEESE GARLIC GRITS

Makes 6 servings

White grits are ground corn from which the yellow outer covering (hull) has been removed; yellow grits are made from corn with the covering (hull) left on. Southerners have always considered white grits to be superior. In antebellum days, dried corn was coarsely grated from the cob with a tool called a "gritter."

They tell a story in the South about a Northern salesman who politely refused the customary breakfast serving of grits, even though there was no extra charge for them. The waitress persisted morning after morning. Finally one day he asked why he should waste good food by taking a serving that he didn't want. She looked him in the eye and said, "Mister, I think it's a law." Maybe it isn't, but it oughta be!

1 cup grits, cooked according to pkg. directions
1 stick (¼ lb.) butter or margarine, cut up or melted
1½ Tbsp. Worcestershire sauce
¾ lb. grated cheddar cheese
1 clove garlic, minced
dash of hot sauce
2 egg whites

1. Cook grits to a thick, but not stiff, consistency.
2. While the grits are still hot, add butter, Worcestershire sauce, cheese, garlic, and hot sauce.
3. Beat egg whites until stiff. Fold into grits.
4. Pour into a greased 2-quart casserole dish.
5. Bake at 400°F for 20 minutes or until light brown on top.

FRIED GRITS

Makes 6 servings

2 cups cooked grits
½ tsp. baking powder (added to grits cooking water)
5 eggs, beaten and divided
½ cup (1 stick) margarine at room temperature
1 tsp. flour
¼ cup milk
vegetable oil

1. Cook grits according to package directions, with baking powder added to the water.
2. When grits are done, stir in two beaten eggs.
3. Add margarine and flour and mix well. Cook 15 minutes longer.
4. Pour the grits mixture into a square baking dish to a depth of about ¾ inch. Cover and refrigerate overnight.
5. Cut the grits into 2-inch squares.
6. In a separate bowl, beat remaining three eggs and milk together. Dip squares into egg mixture and fry in hot oil until golden brown. Turn only one time.
7. Drain and serve hot with butter and honey.

VEGETABLE FRITTERS

Makes 16–20 fritters

The word "fritter," means small cakes of fried batter containing a vegetable or fruit. "Fritter" is derived from the French word friture, meaning something fried, or the fat used for frying. Fritters have been especially popular in the American South where French colonists settled.

When using fresh vegetables, be sure to boil them first in water until they are just tender. Then drain and cool them. When using canned vegetables, for example, whole-kernel corn or creamed corn, do not drain their liquids. Instead, omit the milk called for in the recipe.

You can spice up the fritters you make by adding a small amount of chopped jalapeño pepper. You may also add a small amount of grated cheese to some of the vegetables.

> ½ cup milk
> 1 Tbsp. vegetable oil
> 1 egg
> 1½ cups self-rising flour
> 1 tsp. salt
> 1½ cups vegetables (your choice), cooked until just tender

1. Combine milk and oil.
2. Beat egg until fluffy. Add to milk and oil.
3. Slowly add the flour and salt. Mix well.
4. Stir in vegetable of your choice. Mix well.
5. Drop by spoonfuls into deep, preheated vegetable oil, and deep-fry until golden brown on all sides. Drain on paper towels. Serve hot.

MACARONI AND CHEESE

Makes 6 servings

1½ cups uncooked macaroni (elbows, shells, or spirals)
2½ cups water
3 Tbsp. flour
1½ cups milk, divided
1½ cups cheddar cheese, shredded and divided
½ cup mozzarella cheese, shredded
½ cup (1 stick) margarine at room temperature
salt and pepper to taste
parsley flakes
paprika

1. Cook macaroni in lightly salted water until tender. Remove from heat and drain.
2. Mix together flour and ½ cup milk until all flour is dissolved. Pour remaining cup of milk into a saucepan. Mix in the flour and milk mixture. Cook on medium heat until the mixture begins to thicken.
3. Add ¾ cup cheddar cheese, all the mozzarella cheese, and margarine, blending well.
4. Add salt and pepper.
5. Place drained macaroni into a greased baking dish and pour the sauce over the macaroni. Do not stir. Place the remainder of the cheddar cheese on top. Sprinkle with a small amount of parsley and paprika.
6. Bake in a 350°F oven for 15–20 minutes. (This does not have to bake long because everything is precooked.) Remove from the oven when the top layer of cheese has melted and begins to brown a little.

FRIED OKRA

Makes 4–6 servings

2 lb. fresh okra
½ cup flour
1 cup cornmeal
½ tsp. Cajun seasoning
salt and pepper to taste
vegetable oil

1. Wash okra and trim stem ends. Pat dry and cut into rounds about ½ inch thick.
2. Combine flour, cornmeal, and seasonings. Dredge okra in cornmeal mixture and deep-fry in hot oil. Fry in small batches to keep the pieces from sticking together.

OKRA AND TOMATOES

Makes 6 servings

2 lb. okra
1 onion, chopped
1 green onion, chopped
1 clove garlic, minced
2 Tbsp. vegetable oil
16 oz. can diced tomatoes
½ cup water
½ tsp. Creole seasoning
salt and pepper to taste

1. Wash okra and trim stem ends. Cut into rounds about ½ inch thick.
2. Sauté onions, garlic, and okra in oil for about 10 minutes.
3. Add tomatoes, water, and seasonings. Reduce heat and cook for about 25 minutes, stirring occasionally.
4. Serve over rice.

BARBECUED ONIONS

Makes 2 servings

These go well with anything cooked on the grill.

1 large white onion
2 Tbsp. barbecue sauce
4 Tbsp. flour
1 Tbsp. chili powder
1 Tbsp. margarine

1. Peel onion and slice ¼ inch thick. Separate onion slices into rings.
2. Spread onion rings with barbecue sauce.
3. Combine flour and chili powder.
4. Dust the onion rings with the flour mixture. Place rings on a greased cookie sheet and brush lightly with melted margarine.
5. Bake in a 350°F oven for 25 minutes or until golden brown, turning once.

SMOTHERED ONIONS

Makes 2 servings

1 large onion
1 Tbsp. butter or margarine
½ tsp. garlic powder
salt and pepper to taste
1 tsp. Worcestershire sauce
¼ cup water

1. Peel and cut onion into large pieces.
2. Melt butter in saucepan. Add garlic powder, salt, pepper, and Worcestershire sauce. Mix well. Turn the burner on high. When the butter begins to turn slightly brown, add onions. Stir constantly until onions begin to brown. Turn heat to low.
3. Add water. Place a lid on the pan and let stand on very low heat until ready to serve.

PARBOILED FRIED POTATOES

Makes 4 servings

These are really crunchy on the outside and soft on the inside. My three sons loved them when they were growing up.

2 large potatoes
2½ cups vegetable oil

salt and pepper to taste

1. Peel potatoes and cut into large pieces. Cover with water and boil on medium heat until tender. Drain and set aside to cool.
2. Heat oil in a large pot. Drop dry potatoes into preheated oil and fry until a golden brown. Remove from oil and drain on paper towels.
3. Sprinkle with salt and pepper and serve immediately.

SMOTHERED POTATOES

Makes 4 servings

2 large potatoes
½ tsp. salt
½ tsp. garlic pepper
¼ tsp. lemon pepper

⅛ tsp. cayenne pepper
3 Tbsp. self-rising flour
3 Tbsp. vegetable oil
1 large onion, sliced in rings

1. Peel, rinse and slice potatoes in thin round slices. Blot dry with paper towels.
2. Mix together seasonings and flour. Sprinkle over potatoes in large mixing bowl, tossing well.
3. Heat oil in skillet. Add potatoes, turning often.
4. While potatoes are browning, lower the heat to a low or medium heat. Add onions. Turn frequently with a spatula, being careful not to break the potatoes.
5. When potatoes and onions are brown, place lid on skillet and steam for 20–30 minutes, or until vegetables are tender.
6. Remove lid and turn the burner on high again. Turn vegetables over with spatula frequently, until potatoes are both crunchy and soft—about 5 minutes on high.
7. Remove from stove and serve.

SWEET POTATOES

Sweet potatoes have been a Southern staple forever. More recently, many other people have discovered the great taste and variety of dishes that can be made from the sweet potato that the South has enjoyed for years.

Sweet potatoes are wonderful baked (unpeeled) with nothing added but butter. To bake, just wash the potatoes and dry them well. Place a few drops of vegetable oil in the palm of your hands and rub over the entire surface of the potatoes. Place in a baking pan and bake in a 350°F oven for about 1½ hours. You can determine if a potato is fully cooked by pressing on it. If it is soft, then it is fully cooked. Remove from the oven and peel. Either leave whole or cut into serving slices. Serve with butter.

To fry, peel raw potatoes and cut them into slices. Parboil until tender in lightly salted water. Drain and dry. Deep-fry in preheated vegetable oil. When crispy and brown, remove from oil and drain. Sprinkle with sugar to serve.

Sweet potatoes can also be boiled and whipped with butter and a little milk, exactly the way you make mashed white potatoes.

They can also be grilled, as well as used in pies, cakes, and breads.

Our mother ate sweet potatoes very often and told us many times they were one of the healthiest foods that you could ever eat. And our mother lived to be almost ninety-eight years of age!

CANDIED SWEET POTATOES

Makes 6 servings

8 medium-sized sweet potatoes
2 cups water
salt to taste
1 cup granulated sugar
1 cup brown sugar
2 Tbsp. butter
1 slice lemon
1 tsp. cinnamon
½ tsp. nutmeg

1. Peel potatoes and cut in half lengthwise. Boil in lightly salted water for 10 minutes. Remove potatoes from water (reserve cooking water) and place in greased casserole dish.
2. To the water in which the potatoes were boiled, add sugars, butter, lemon, cinnamon, and nutmeg. Cover and simmer for at least 30 minutes, until it has the consistency of a light syrup. Pour over sweet potatoes
3. Bake at 325°F until syrup becomes heavier and potatoes are tender.

SWEET POTATO CASSEROLE

Makes 6 servings

3 cups sweet potatoes
1½ cups brown sugar
2 eggs, well beaten
½ tsp. salt
1½ tsp. vanilla
half stick (4 Tbsp.) margarine, melted
½ cup milk
½ cup white raisins

Topping:
    ½ cup brown sugar
    ⅓ cup self-rising flour
    ½ cup (1 stick) margarine, melted
    1 cup pecans, chopped

1. Boil or bake potatoes until tender. Peel, mash well, and set aside.
2. Combine 1½ cups brown sugar, eggs, salt, vanilla, half stick margarine, and milk. Beat well. Stir in raisins. Add the potatoes and mix thoroughly.
3. Pour into a greased baking dish.
4. To make the topping, combine ½ cup brown sugar and flour thoroughly. Add one stick melted margarine slowly, mixing well. Add pecans and mix. Sprinkle over the entire top of potato mixture.
5. Bake at 375°F for 40 minutes.

BAKED SQUASH

Makes 6 servings

5 lb. medium-sized yellow squash
¼ cup chopped onion
3 Tbsp. butter
2 eggs
2 tsp. salt
½ tsp. pepper
1 cup bread crumbs

1. Cut off tips of squash, wash, and cut into pieces. Place in a saucepan with lightly salted water just to cover. Cook until tender. Drain and mash.
2. Sauté onion in butter until transparent and add to the squash.
3. Beat eggs and add to mixture.
4. Add salt, pepper, and bread crumbs. Reserve about 1 Tbsp. of crumbs for topping. Spoon vegetable mixture into greased casserole dish and sprinkle 1 Tbsp. crumbs over.
5. Bake at 350°F for about 25 minutes.

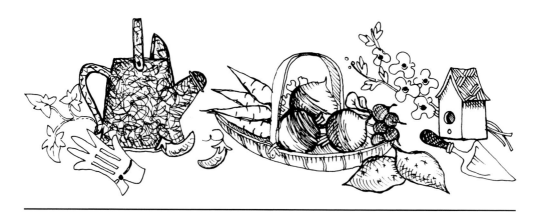

FRIED GREEN TOMATOES

Makes 4 servings

In the fall when frost was just about to put an end to the tomato crop for the year, cooks would gather all tomatoes that had not ripened. They pickled some for use in the winter, but some inventive person was smart enough to try frying them. What a treat!

3 medium-sized green tomatoes
salt and pepper to taste
2 cups self-rising flour
1 cup vegetable oil

1. Wash surfaces of tomatoes and remove stems. Slice in round slices about ¼ inch thick.
2. Sprinkle salt and pepper on both sides.
3. Roll each slice in flour and place in a large bowl.
4. Drizzle tap water on them until they are gooey.
5. Roll them a second time in flour
6. Fry in preheated oil over medium heat. Turn often. When tomatoes are a golden brown, remove from oil and drain.

Note:
   The tomatoes are best for frying when they are just beginning to show a little pink in the skin. Do not peel the tomatoes for frying.

Meat, Poultry, and Fish

BEEF BRISKET

3–4 lb. beef brisket
1 tsp. meat tenderizer
1 tsp. salt
½ tsp. lemon pepper
½ cup Worcestershire sauce
½ cup liquid smoke

1. Wash brisket and trim off excess fat. Rub a little meat tenderizer on both sides of meat and let stand 15–20 minutes.
2. Rub a small amount of salt and lemon pepper all over meat. Place meat in a foil-lined baking dish.
3. Pour the Worcestershire sauce and liquid smoke over the brisket. Close foil up over the top and seal as tightly as possible. Place in the refrigerator overnight.
4. Bake at 350°F for at least 3–4 hours. Remove from oven and pour off all but ½ cup juice.

Note:
Thinly sliced, leftover brisket is great for hot or cold sandwiches. Or you can chop the meat, add barbecue sauce, heat the mixture, and serve it on buns. You can also use leftover beef in homemade vegetable soup or a stew.

COUNTRY BRISKET

3–4 lb. beef brisket
liquid smoke
1½ lb. brown sugar
1 tsp. black pepper
1 tsp. garlic powder
1 tsp. meat tenderizer
1 tsp. seasoned salt

1. The day before you cook the brisket, rub meat with liquid smoke.
2. In a large container, combine sugar, pepper, garlic powder, meat tenderizer, and seasoned salt.
3. Add brisket and rub mixture into the meat. Let set overnight.
4. Put meat in a smoker about 3 or 4 feet from the coals and allow to cook for at least 4 hours.
5. When tender, slice, and serve.

A'DOBE

Makes 8–10 servings

2–3 lb. round steak, cut
1½ inches thick (you may have
    to request this special thick
    cut from your butcher)
salt and pepper to taste
½ cup vegetable oil
4 Tbsp. self-rising flour
1 cup onion, chopped
1 bell pepper, chopped
2 ribs celery, chopped

2 cloves garlic, minced
¼ cup parsley flakes
1 can beef broth
1 can water
1 Tbsp. ketchup
1 small bay leaf
2 whole cloves
2 whole allspice
1 rutabaga or turnip
2 Tbsp. red cooking sherry

1. Cut steak into two or three pieces. Sprinkle a small amount of salt and pepper over each piece.
2. Pour oil into a preheated Dutch oven or similar pot. Place steak into hot oil and stir constantly until browned. Add flour and stir.
3. Add onion, bell pepper, celery, garlic, parsley flakes, beef broth, water, ketchup, bay leaf, cloves, and allspice. Boil, stirring frequently, for approximately one hour on medium heat.
4. Cut the turnip or rutabaga in fourths, stir into pot, and continue cooking until vegetable is tender. Remove the rutabaga or turnip and discard. (It is added for flavor only.)
5. Add cooking sherry. Continue cooking for 5 minutes.
6. Salt and pepper to taste.
7. Total cooking time is about one hour and 45 minutes. Serve over rice.

Note:

    Cut a circle of cheesecloth, and place the bay leaf (broken into three pieces), cloves, and allspice into the center. Pull up sides and tie with a thin strip of cheesecloth. This will enable you to remove them easily from the A'dobe. If you drop the spices in loose, they are hard to find later to remove them.

OVEN-BAKED RUMP ROAST

rump roast (your choice of size)
2 cloves garlic (sliced lengthwise)
2 tsp. Worcestershire sauce
salt and pepper to taste
paprika to taste
¼ cup vegetable oil
3 Tbsp. self-rising flour
½ cup water
1 can beef broth

1. Using a very sharp knife, punch holes into the roast and insert the garlic slices. I call this step, stuffing the roast with garlic.
2. Rub the Worcestershire sauce on all sides of the roast.
3. Mix together the salt, pepper, and paprika and rub on all sides of the roast.
4. Pour vegetable oil in an oven-proof roaster. Place on stove burner and heat oil. Place the roast into the hot oil, turning constantly until it is seared or dark brown over the entire surface.
5. Place the lid on the roaster and put into a 350°F oven. Check every 30 minutes to make sure it is not cooking dry and to turn the roast over. Bake for a total of approximately 2 hours. Baking time depends on the size of the roast. The internal temperature should be 135–140°F. You should not have to add water, but if your roast juices do cook dry, just add about a cup of water.
6. When the roast is tender, remove from oven, place in a covered baking dish, and keep warm in the oven.
7. Mix the flour and water until all lumps are dissolved and it looks like milk.
8. Add one can of beef broth and one can of water to the pan drippings. Bring to a boil.
9. Add the flour-water mixture while stirring constantly. Some lumps may appear. Don't worry, they will dissolve or you may remove them. Cook the gravy for approximately 10–15 minutes.
10. Season with salt and pepper.
11. If gravy is too thick, add more beef broth. If it's too thin, add more flour-water mixture. This is the tastiest gravy ever!

CHICKEN-FRIED STEAK

Makes 6 servings

2 lb. round steak
meat tenderizer
2 cups self-rising flour
salt and pepper to taste
paprika to taste
1 cup buttermilk
2 cups vegetable oil

1. Rinse steak well. Sprinkle with meat tenderizer and pound until thin.
2. Combine flour, salt, pepper, and paprika.
3. Pour buttermilk into separate bowl.
4. Dredge steak in flour, dip into buttermilk, then dredge again in the flour.
5. Fry in oil until golden brown. It doesn't take very long for the meat to fry!
6. You may want to sprinkle the cooked meat with a small amount of salt while hot. But remember that the meat tenderizer is salty, so use additional salt sparingly.
7. Serve the steak with the following gravy.

Gravy:
Pour off all except ¼ cup drippings from skillet. Stir in **3 Tbsp. flour** along with **salt and pepper to taste**. Add about **2 cups milk**. Stir constantly with fork or wire whisk until smooth and thick. Serve over steak.

STOVE-TOP POT ROAST

Makes 8–10 servings

3 lb. chuck roast
½ tsp. meat tenderizer
1–2 slices lemon
½ tsp. salt
½ tsp. black pepper
½ tsp. paprika
1 tsp. Worcestershire sauce
½ cup vegetable oil
4 Tbsp. self-rising flour
1 can beef broth
1 can water
¼ cup parsley flakes

2 onions, peeled and quartered
1 bell pepper, cut into 2-inch strips
2 ribs celery, cut into 2-inch
   strips
2 cloves garlic, chopped
3–4 medium carrots, cut into
   pieces
3 medium potatoes, peeled and
   cut into 2-inch chunks
1 can, or 10 fresh mushrooms
¼ cup red cooking wine

1. Rinse roast with water and pat dry with paper towel.
2. Rub the meat tenderizer thoroughly over all sides of the roast.
3. Squeeze the lemon slices over all sides and rub into meat.
4. Mix together salt, pepper, and paprika and rub over all sides of roast.
5. Cut meat into 3-inch squares. Toss gently in large bowl to make sure all sides are seasoned.
6. Drop a few drops of Worcestershire sauce over roast pieces. Let stand for 10 minutes.
7. Heat the oil in a Dutch oven on the stove top. When oil is hot, spoon the roast in. Turn frequently until all pieces are well browned and all liquid has stopped seeping from meat.
8. Add the flour and stir well. Continue stirring until floured meat has browned.
9. Add the beef broth and one can of water.
10. Cook for one hour over medium heat until meat is tender. Add a little water as meat cooks to maintain a semi-thick gravy consistency.
11. After boiling for an hour to an hour and a half, turn the burner down so that the pot is simmering but not boiling. Add the parsley flakes and stir well.
12. Place the onions, bell pepper, celery, garlic, carrots, potatoes, and mushrooms on top of roast. Pour the cooking wine over top. Do not stir. Place cover on Dutch oven and continue to simmer for about 45 minutes.
13. Remove vegetables and place in a separate serving dish.
14. Take about 2 or 3 Tbsp. of roast gravy and drizzle over the vegetables.
15. Serve the roast and gravy over rice.

GRILLED STEAK

What can I say? There are so many backyard steak cooks that it would make you dizzy to try to list all of the various methods and marinades that people use—beer, whiskey, wine, whatever. If you are going to pay the price for beef, you should at least try to make the steak taste good. Start with good meat—sirloin, T-bone, ribeye—then try this!

Steak should be 1–1½ inches thick. Thin steaks do not grill well. Start your fire—the hotter the better. Punch holes in the steak with a fork and add the following: **black pepper, onion powder, garlic powder, a sprinkling of Worcestershire sauce, and seasoned salt**. Rub in good. Place steak on grill and cook for 10 minutes. Turn over and cook for another 10 minutes on the other side. Do not overcook. If you smear real **butter** on the steak before cooking, it will enhance the taste.

PEPPER STEAK

Makes 4–6 servings

2 lb. chuck steak
salt and pepper to taste
1 cup flour
2 Tbsp. vegetable oil
2 green bell peppers
1 large onion

14½ oz. can stewed tomatoes
1 Tbsp. Worcestershire sauce
chopped parsley
1 beef bouillon cube
1 bay leaf

1. Cut meat into serving-size pieces.
2. Sprinkle with salt and pepper. Dredge in flour.
3. In hot oil in deep skillet, brown steak on each side. Remove.
4. Slice peppers and onions into thin strips. Place half of pepper strips and half of onion slices in bottom of Dutch oven or roaster. Arrange steak on top. Cover with remaining pepper and onion.
5. Mix together tomatoes, Worcestershire sauce, parsley, crumbled bouillon cube, and bay leaf. Pour over meat and vegetables.
6. Bake covered at 300°F for about 45 minutes or until steak is tender.
7. Remove bay leaf and serve over rice.

SMOTHERED STEAK AND GRAVY

Makes 4–6 servings

meat tenderizer
2–3 lb. round steak
1 Tbsp. Worcestershire sauce
2–3 Tbsp. vegetable oil
2–3 Tbsp. self-rising flour
1 large onion, sliced in rings
2 cloves garlic, minced
2 cans beef broth
2 Tbsp. parsley flakes
salt and pepper to taste

1. Sprinkle a small amount of meat tenderizer on both sides of steak. Let stand for 5 minutes. Cut into 2–3-inch squares.
2. Sprinkle Worcestershire sauce on the steak and rub it over the surface.
3. Heat the oil in a skillet. When the oil is hot, drop the steak into the oil and brown, turning often. Brown to a dark color. Right before the steak appears to burn, add flour and stir quickly.
4. Add onions and garlic. Stir until they are well coated with oil and flour.
5. Add beef broth, parsley, salt, and pepper. Cook for approximately 30 minutes on a medium boil. Reduce heat to simmer and leave alone until ready to serve. The gravy will not be thick. If you want a thicker gravy, add more flour to the browning step, or use less broth.

STEAK ROLL

Makes 6–8 slices

2–3 lb. round steak, boneless
1 Tbsp. melted butter
½ tsp. Worcestershire sauce
½ tsp. lemon juice

1. Rinse steak with cold water and blot dry.
2. Combine the butter, Worcestershire sauce, and lemon juice. Rub into both sides of the steak.
3. Lay the steak out on a cutting board and tenderize with a meat chopper. If you do not have one, use a small saucer turned edgewise and pound the steak. Use a saucer that will not break. Set the steak aside.

Filling:
    ½ cup onion, minced
    ½ cup bell pepper, minced
    ½ cup celery, minced
    1 clove garlic, minced
    2 Tbsp. parsley, minced
    1 egg, hard-cooked and chopped fine
    ½ cup toast squares
    1 Tbsp. lemon juice
    ⅛ tsp. salt
    ⅛ tsp. black pepper
    2 Tbsp. melted butter
    ¼ cup beef broth or water

1. Combine all ingredients except beef broth. Mix well.
2. Spread mixture over the steak. Press down with your hand. Take one end of steak and roll into a log. The filling should stay in place. Tie log with a baking string. Place in a baking dish uncovered.
3. Bake in a 425°F oven until the top is brown.
4. Add beef broth or water. Cover with a lid and bake for 45 minutes at 325°F.
5. When ready to serve, slice crosswise. Spoon some of the drippings over top.

PAN-BROILED STEAK OR CHICKEN

You choose the meat. I cook minute steaks, rib-eyes, T-bones, or chicken parts the same way.

Wash meat and blot dry. On beef, you may want to sprinkle a small amount of **meat tenderizer** on both sides and let stand for 5–10 minutes. If you use meat tenderizer, do not use salt. The meat tenderizer is salty enough. Sprinkle **lemon pepper** on all surfaces. Rub a mixture of **Worcestershire sauce** and **liquid smoke** on surfaces of meat.

In a large heavy skillet, preheat **2 Tbsp. vegetable oil**. Pack the meat into the hot oil and turn frequently from side to side in order to brown. Once the meat is a dark brown, turn burner down to low heat. Chicken should cook on low heat until tender. Steaks vary to the individual taste, well done or rare.

Remove meat from oil. Drain off excess oil. Place skillet back on a medium heat and add ¼ cup water. Bring to a heavy boil, scraping the sediment from the bottom of the pan. When ready to serve the chicken or steak, pour a couple of spoonfuls of the liquid over the meat.

SMOTHERED PORK RIBS

Makes 6 servings

Our mother's recipe.

2–3 lb. pork ribs
2 Tbsp. Worcestershire sauce
3–4 Tbsp. vegetable oil
3–4 Tbsp. flour
1 onion, chopped
1 Tbsp. parsley flakes
2 cloves garlic, chopped
1 small bay leaf
1 can beef broth
1 can water
salt and pepper to taste

1. Rinse and cut ribs into individual serving sizes.
2. Sprinkle with Worcestershire sauce. Let stand for 5 minutes.
3. Heat oil in a large heavy pot. Brown ribs in hot oil, turning over and over in the pot in order to brown all sides. When ribs are really brown, remove pot from burner and remove ribs.
4. Place the pot back on the burner and add the flour, stirring constantly, scraping all the sediment from the bottom of the pot.
5. When the flour is browned, add the onions, parsley, garlic, and bay. Stir well.
6. Add beef broth and water. Bring to a hard boil.
7. Add ribs, salt, and pepper. If the gravy is too thick, add more water. Turn down heat and simmer for one hour. Serve over rice.

BABY BACK PORK RIBS

Makes 6 servings

1 tsp. black pepper
1 tsp. cayenne pepper
1 Tbsp. seasoned salt
2 Tbsp. Worcestershire sauce
2 lb. baby back pork ribs
mesquite or hickory chips
your favorite barbecue sauce

1. Combine peppers, salt, and Worcestershire sauce. Rub into ribs. Place in covered roasting pan.
2. Bake at 225°F for 1½ hours. Let stand for 30 minutes or until cool enough to handle.
3. Place on the barbecue grill and smoke for 45 minutes, using mesquite or hickory chips.
4. Baste with your favorite barbecue sauce and cook for another 30 minutes. Avoid direct heat. Baste one final time before serving.

FAJITAS

Makes 6 servings

2–3 lb. skirt steak

Marinade:
    ¼ cup lime juice
    ¼ cup tequila
    2 Tbsp. olive oil
    2 cloves garlic, minced
    1 fresh jalapeño pepper, minced
    1 Tbsp. cilantro, chopped
    ½ tsp. salt
    ½ tsp. black pepper

12 flour tortillas

Condiments:
    2 onions, sliced and cooked lightly in butter
    guacamole
    salsa and/or pico de gallo
    sour cream
    cheese

1. Trim fat from steak and remove as many of the tough membranes as you can.
2. Combine all marinade ingredients in a bowl. Pour over beef. Cover and refrigerate for 8 hours, turning meat several times.
3. Wrap the tortillas in foil and place on side of hot grill to warm.
4. Place the meat on greased grill rack, 4–6 inches above the coals. Reserve the marinade. Cook for about 10–12 minutes (or until done to your taste), turning once and basting frequently with the marinade.
5. To serve, cut the meat across the grain into thin slices and place on warm platter.
6. Serve tortillas and condiments in separate dishes. Place a few strips of meat and several of the condiments in each tortilla and fold. Allow two fajitas per person.

HAMBURGER STEAK

Makes 4 servings

1 lb. ground chuck
1 chopped onion, divided
half a bell pepper, chopped
2 ribs celery, chopped
¼ cup parsley flakes
1 egg, beaten

½ cup crushed butter crackers
⅛ tsp. garlic powder
⅛ tsp. red pepper
½ tsp. salt
1 tsp. vegetable oil

1. Mix all ingredients thoroughly except half the onion and the 1 tsp. oil.
2. Form meat mixture into strips 3–4 inches long and about 1 inch thick.
3. Heat oil in a frying pan. Place hamburger steaks into the hot oil and brown on both sides, turning frequently.
4. When meat is very brown on all sides, place remaining onion on top and around the steaks. Turn heat to simmer. Cover pan and continue to simmer for approximately 45 minutes. A sauce should accumulate in the pan. If it doesn't, add ¼ cup water and mix with onions.
5. Serve onion sauce on top of steak.

"Country-style" or "old-fashioned" hams are usually dry-cured by rubbing the meat with salt and spices and then smoking them slowly. This process makes the ham very salty. To remove some of the salty taste, scrub the ham all over in very hot water, and then boil in fresh water for about 1 hour before actually cooking the ham.

Another way to reduce the salt content before cooking is to submerge a country ham in water and then place it in the refrigerator to soak for about 8 hours. It is then ready to be baked at 325°F for 25–30 minutes per pound.

Because these hams retain a lot of their salty flavor, they are usually sliced almost paper-thin for eating.

Wet-cured hams are preserved by soaking the meat in a solution of water, sugar, salt, and spices. Wet-cured hams are the most common and popular because they are not so salty as the dry-cured ones.

Curing—and even cooking—fresh hams is becoming a thing of the past because fully cooked hams are so readily available today. This is an old Southern recipe for boiled fresh ham.

FRESH HAM

Allow ½ lb. per serving

8 cups cold water
8 cups apple cider
3 carrots, quartered
4 onions, quartered
2 cloves garlic

4 celery ribs with leaves
8 peppercorns
1 Tbsp. dry mustard
6 whole cloves
10–15 lb. ham

1. Place all ingredients except ham in large pot and bring to a rolling boil. Lower heat and simmer for 30 minutes.
2. Place ham into the boiling sauce. Cover and simmer on low heat for 25–30 minutes per pound. Let the ham cool slightly in the liquid.
3. Remove the skin while still hot (as soon as you can comfortably handle the ham).
4. Glaze the ham just like you would a precooked one (see glazes below), or slice it and serve it as is.

Pineapple Glaze:
　　whole cloves
　　1 can pineapple slices
　　1 cup brown sugar
　　1 tsp. ground cloves

1. Score the precooked ham (do not remove the skin), making diamond shapes. Place ham in large baking pan.
2. Insert a clove in the center of each diamond.
3. Drain pineapple slices, reserving juice.
4. Blend pineapple juice with brown sugar and ground cloves. Pour over ham.
5. Bake ham uncovered in 350°F oven, basting every 15 minutes with pan juices. Bake 20–25 minutes per pound. About 30 minutes before ham is heated through, garnish with pineapple slices and continue basting.

Honey Glaze:
　　¼ cup dark corn syrup
　　1 cup honey
　　½ cup butter

1. Place precooked ham in large baking pan. Place uncovered in oven heated to 350°F. Bake 20–25 minutes per pound.

2. Heat the glaze ingredients in the top of a double boiler. Keep warm while ham is baking.
3. About halfway through cooking the ham, begin basting with the glaze every 15 minutes. During the last 10 minutes of baking, turn oven very high to caramelize the glaze.

Marmalade Glaze:
    1 cup orange marmalade (or any jelly you prefer)
    ½ cup brown sugar
    1 cup brown mustard
    3 Tbsp. cider vinegar
    pinch of ground cloves

1. Place precooked ham in large baking pan. Place uncovered in oven heated to 350°F. Bake 20–25 minutes per pound.
2. Heat the marmalade and sugar over a low flame to dissolve the sugar.
3. When the sugar is dissolved, remove from heat and stir in the mustard, vinegar, and cloves.
4. About halfway through cooking the ham, begin basting with the glaze. Baste every 15 minutes until ham is done.

Cajun Glaze:
    1 cup cane syrup
    1 cup spicy brown mustard
    ½ cup brown sugar
    1 tsp. black pepper
    ½ tsp. cinnamon
    ½ tsp. ground cloves
    ½ tsp. nutmeg
    ½ tsp. gumbo file

1. Place precooked ham, uncovered, in large baking pan. Place in 350°F oven and bake 20–25 minutes per pound.
2. Mix all glaze ingredients and brush over ham before baking and at 15-minute intervals while the ham is baking.

Ham with Crust:
1. Before placing precooked ham in 350°F oven, brush meat with well beaten egg. Bake ham, uncovered, 20–25 minutes per pound.
2. During the last 30 minutes of baking time, sprinkle meat with plain or sugared bread crumbs.

FRIED MEAT PIES

Makes 6–8 pies

1½ lb. lean ground beef	1 Tbsp. salt
1½ lb. ground pork	1 tsp. black pepper
1 cup onions, chopped	1 tsp. cayenne pepper
3 green onions, chopped	⅓ cup all-purpose flour

1. Combine and cook the beef, pork, onions, and seasonings until the meat loses its pink color.
2. Sift flour over the meat mixture, stirring constantly. Let cool. Drain off excess drippings.
3. Set aside and follow directions for the crust recipe below.

Crust:
   ⅓ cup shortening
   2 cups self-rising flour
   1 egg, beaten
   ¾ cup milk
   vegetable oil

1. Cut shortening into flour with pastry blender or two forks.
2. Add egg and milk, mixing until you can knead the dough into a ball.
3. Roll out one-third of the dough at a time on a floured surface. Cut into two or three 5-inch circles.
4. Place 1 Tbsp. filling on one-half of a dough circle. Dip your fingertips into water and then use them to dampen the edge of the circle. Fold empty dough half over the meat mixture to form a half-circle pocket. Crimp edges with a fork dipped in water.
5. Fry in hot vegetable oil (enough to cover well) until golden brown on both sides.

Note:
   If you prefer to bake instead of fry, use two circles of dough for each pie. Place 2 Tbsp. of meat mixture in the center of a circle and cover with a second circle of dough on top.
   Moisten and seal edges the same as above. Brush tops with melted butter. Place on baking sheet and bake in a 375°F oven for 25 minutes or until golden brown.

STUFFED GREEN PEPPERS

Makes 4 servings

4 medium or large green bell peppers
1 lb. lean ground beef
½ cup onion, chopped
½ cup bell pepper, chopped
1 jalapeño pepper, seeded and chopped
1 tsp. salt
1 small can chopped mushrooms
1 Tbsp. ketchup
½ tsp. hot sauce
1 Tbsp. barbecue sauce
1–1½ cups cooked rice
mozzarella cheese, shredded
cheddar cheese, shredded
½ cup butter crackers, crushed

1. Remove cores from four bell peppers, clean out the seeds, and rinse. Cut each pepper in half.
2. Drop peppers into boiling water to cover and simmer 5 minutes.
3. In a frying pan, cook ground beef until lightly browned.
4. Add onion, chopped pepper, jalapeño pepper, and salt. Sauté until vegetables are tender.
5. Add mushrooms, ketchup, hot sauce, barbecue sauce, and rice.
6. Remove peppers from water and place them cut side up in a well-greased baking pan. Fill each pepper to capacity with the meat mixture. Top with a mixture of the two cheeses.
7. Bake at 350°F for approximately 10 minutes.
8. Remove from oven and sprinkle with cracker crumbs.

LIVER AND ONIONS

Makes 4 servings

1½ lb. calf's liver
1 tsp. salt
½ tsp. black pepper
2 Tbsp. flour
½ cup vegetable oil
1½ cups water
2 large onions, sliced

1. Cut the liver into serving-size pieces.
2. Sprinkle with salt and pepper. Dredge in flour.
3. In a heavy skillet, brown quickly in about ½ inch of oil. Remove from skillet and pour off excess oil.
4. Add leftover flour to the pan drippings. Stir and scrape bottom of pan.
5. Add water and stir up sediment to make gravy. Put the liver back in the gravy and lay onion slices on top of the liver.
6. Cover the skillet and simmer for about 15 minutes.

MEAT LOAF

Makes 10 slices, about 5–6 servings

1 lb. ground beef
¼ lb. pure pork sausage
1 egg
¼ cup onion, chopped
¼ cup bell pepper, chopped
¼ cup celery, chopped
1 clove garlic, minced
2 Tbsp. parsley flakes
1 cup crushed cheese crackers
1 tsp. salt
¼ tsp. black pepper
1 can steak mushroom gravy
half can water

1. Combine ground beef, pork sausage, egg, onion, bell pepper, celery, garlic, parsley, cracker crumbs, salt, and pepper. Mix well. Shape into a loaf and place into a greased baking dish.
2. Mix gravy and water. Pour over top of meat loaf.
3. Bake at 350°F for approximately an hour, basting often. If the juices seem to be drying up, add ¼ cup more water.

Notes:

1. I use hot pork sausage. You can use the brand of your choice and it does not have to be hot.

2. Instead of the steak gravy, you can use a can of tomato sauce. You can also choose not to top the meat loaf with any sauce at all. If you do not bake it with a sauce, the meat is great eaten over creamed potatoes.

DOUBLE-DIPPED FRIED CHICKEN (NORMA'S SPECIALTY)

Makes 4–5 servings

My three sons request this fried chicken on every visit to our home.

about 1 lb. self-rising flour
chicken, cut up into pieces
salt
black pepper
paprika
vegetable oil

1. Pour flour into large mixing bowl.
2. Clean chicken pieces. Sprinkle salt, pepper, and paprika all over the chicken.
3. Place chicken one piece at a time into the flour, coating well. Place into another large mixing bowl. Once you have floured all the chicken, sprinkle tap water over the chicken while tossing it around in the bowl. When the chicken becomes really gooey and runny, take one piece at a time and coat again in the first bowl of flour.
4. Drop chicken one piece at a time into preheated deep fryer. Fry until the meat turns a golden brown. Legs and breast pieces take a little longer to cook. Don't get the oil too hot or the meat will darken on the outside and not be cooked on the inside. (Reserve oil and drippings for Fried Chicken Gravy, on the next page.)
5. Drain on paper towels and place in a warm oven until ready to serve.

Note:
   The chicken stays crunchy even when it gets cold!

FRIED CHICKEN GRAVY

3–4 Tbsp. flour
½ cup chopped onion
1 can chicken broth
1 can water
salt and pepper to taste

1. After you have fried the chicken, pour off all oil from the deep fryer, except reserve ¼ cup. Keep that ¼ cup oil, plus all the crunchies and flour settlement in the bottom. Transfer to a skillet.
2. Add flour and brown.
3. Add onion and stir well. Simmer for 3–4 minutes.
4. Stir in chicken broth and water. Season to taste.
5. Cook until onions are tender.
6. Serve over rice or creamed potatoes.

CORNMEAL GRAVY

¼ cup meat drippings (chicken, steak, or pork chops)
4 Tbsp. cornmeal, plain or self-rising
2 Tbsp. flour
1½ cups whole milk
1 cup water
salt and pepper to taste

1. Heat the drippings in a heavy skillet. When the drippings begin to get hot, stir in the cornmeal and flour. Keep stirring until very brown.
2. Mix milk and water and slowly add to the flour and oil mixture, stirring constantly.
3. Continue to stir until the gravy is smooth and of the consistency you like.
4. Add salt and pepper.

COUNTRY TOMATO GRAVY

This is an old Southern recipe for gravy. Many people used to grind their own corn so the supply of cornmeal was much more plentiful than wheat flour.

Makes 8 servings

3 Tbsp. vegetable oil	1 can stewed tomatoes
3 Tbsp. self-rising flour	½ Tbsp. parsley, chopped
½ cup onion, chopped	½ jalapeño pepper, *optional*
¼ cup bell pepper, chopped	3 tomato cans water
¼ cup celery, chopped	salt and pepper to taste
1 clove garlic, minced	½ tsp. Kitchen Bouquet, *optional*

1. Heat oil in a large frying pan. Add flour and cook to a dark brown, stirring constantly.
2. Add onion, bell pepper, celery, and garlic. Stir and cook until mixed well.
3. Add tomatoes, parsley, and jalapeño pepper. Cook at a slow to medium boil, adding water until you get it to the thickness that you want. (You might not use all three cans of water.)
4. Add salt and pepper.
5. Cook until all ingredients are tender. If your flour did not brown properly, you can add the Kitchen Bouquet. When fully cooked, serve over rice or homemade biscuits.

Note:
To get that extra zing, peel, finely chop two fresh ripe tomatoes, and stir into the mix in Step 3. They make a dramatic difference in the gravy's flavor.

Option:
When you have finished cooking the gravy, add a cup or two of peeled cooked shrimp. Then mix the rice and gravy together for a whole different taste. It's great!

MIKE'S CHICKEN

Makes 6 servings

4 large chicken breasts, boneless and skinless
8 Tbsp. butter
8 oz. mozzarella cheese
¼ cup chopped parsley
¼ cup chopped onion
milk, for dipping chicken
fine bread crumbs
½ cup vegetable oil
½ cup or more white wine

1. Cut each breast in half. Pound the chicken with a meat mallet until it is about ¼ inch thick. Each piece should be 4–5 inches in diameter.
2. In the middle of each breast, put 1 Tbsp. butter, 1 oz. cheese, 1 tsp. parsley, and 1 tsp. chopped onion.
3. Fold all four sides of the chicken over to the center, enclosing the cheese and butter mixture. Fasten with toothpicks to hold in place.
4. Dip the chicken in the milk and then in the bread crumbs to coat well.
5. Heat the vegetable oil in a heavy skillet and lightly brown the chicken. Place in a baking dish.
6. Sprinkle white wine liberally over the chicken.
7. Bake at 350°F for 35 minutes or until chicken is cooked through.

CHICKEN AND DUMPLINGS

Makes 6 servings

Years ago chicken and dumplings was a favorite food at country weddings. Serving it was so common that instead of asking, "When are you two going to get married?", the question became, "When are we going to have chicken and dumplings?"

3 chicken breasts
1 medium onion, chopped
salt and pepper to taste
1 can chicken broth
1 can chicken gravy

Dumplings:
    2–3 cups self-rising flour
    2 level Tbsp. butter-flavored shortening
    ½ cup buttermilk

1. Place chicken breasts in enough water to cover, bringing to a medium boil.
2. Add chopped onion, salt, and pepper. Boil on medium heat for approximately 30–40 minutes or until chicken is well done.
3. Remove chicken from broth, debone, cut into small pieces, and set aside. Reserve broth.
4. Add can of chicken broth to the homemade broth and set aside.
5. To make dumplings, place 2–3 cups flour into large mixing bowl.
6. Make a dent in the center of the flour. Place 2 Tbsp. shortening in dent and slowly add buttermilk. Use a fork to blend with flour and shortening. Mix to the consistency of biscuit dough and form into a ball. (You need to work more flour into this mixture than you do for homemade biscuits. See page 201.)
7. Place ball of dough on a floured surface and roll out as thin as you can. Cut into strips.
8. Add chicken back to the broth and bring to a medium boil.
9. Add the dumplings one at a time until you have as many as you want, or until they do not sink when you drop them into the broth.
10. Add the can of chicken gravy and carefully stir. You do not ever want to stir dumplings too much because they will break apart and become mushy. When you have added all the dumplings, turn heat as low as you can get it until ready to serve.

LOUISIANA FRIED TURKEY

Makes 15–18 servings

12–14 lb. turkey
1 bottle liquid garlic
1 bottle liquid onion juice
1 stick (¼ lb.) margarine, melted
1 tsp. Cajun seasoning
4 Tbsp. Worcestershire sauce
salt and pepper to taste
3 Tbsp. hot sauce
2 onions
2 tsp. paprika
2½ gallons peanut oil

1. Wash, dry, and season turkey 2 days before you are ready to fry. To season, combine garlic and onion juices, margarine, Cajun seasoning, Worcestershire sauce, salt, pepper, and hot sauce. Using a large syringe (you can buy a cattle syringe at a farm supply store), inject the turkey all over.
2. Put the onions inside the turkey. Season the outside of the turkey with paprika. After seasoning, allow the turkey to rest for 2 hours at room temperature. Refrigerate for 2 days to marinate before cooking.
3. Heat oil to 350°–375°F in a 20-gallon pot. Place the turkey in hot oil and fry. Cook 3–4 minutes per pound. Turkey will sink until it is done. When it begins to float, cook for 10 more minutes, then remove, carve, and serve.

BARBECUED TURKEY

Makes 15–18 servings

12–14 lb. turkey
¼ cup Worcestershire sauce
1 Tbsp. rosemary
1 tsp. cayenne pepper
1 tsp. black pepper
1 Tbsp. seasoned salt
2 cups favorite barbecue sauce

1. If the turkey is frozen, be sure to remove the neck and giblet packet before preparing the meat. To prepare the turkey, cut away any excess fatty skin and cut off the wing tips. Save both for the giblet gravy. With a sharp knife, slit skin (2-inch cuts) over the whole turkey, spaced about 2 inches apart, being careful not to cut into the meat.
2. Rub Worcestershire sauce over the entire turkey.
3. Combine rosemary, cayenne, black pepper, and seasoned salt. Rub over the turkey.
4. Pull the wings to the back of the turkey and tie down with a cotton string. If you use a rotisserie, be sure that the turkey is balanced and will turn smoothly. If you use a smoker, turn the turkey often. Use hickory or mesquite chips that have been soaked in water. Do not cook over direct heat for the first 3 hours. If you want to catch the drippings, place a cookie sheet on the next lower rack. Replace chips when smoke stops coming out of the cooking vents.
5. Baste with barbecue sauce after turkey has smoked for about 3 hours.
6. Cook the last hour over direct heat to ensure that meat is done. Do not baste during that last hour to allow the turkey to brown.

The total cooking process should take between 5 and 6 hours. The finished turkey should be a dark golden brown. Watch for any sign of dryness, being careful not to overcook the meat.

BAKED CHICKEN OR TURKEY WITH DRESSING AND GIBLET GRAVY

Makes 6 servings

1 whole chicken hen *or* 1 whole turkey
¼ cup lemon juice
2 Tbsp. Worcestershire sauce
salt and pepper to taste
¼ tsp. paprika
2–3 Tbsp. vegetable oil

1. Rinse poultry thoroughly on the inside as well as the outside. Pat dry.
2. Rub the lemon juice over the entire surface.
3. Rub the Worcestershire sauce over the entire surface.
4. Sprinkle entire surface with salt, pepper, and paprika, then rub in seasonings well.
5. Pour oil into oven roaster and heat on the top of the stove. Place poultry into hot oil and turn over constantly until it becomes a medium brown
6. Place lid on roaster and place into a 350°F oven. The poultry will cook in its own juices. Roast for 1 hour, and then reduce heat to 300°F.

The length of roasting time depends on the size of the bird. If it is large, you may have to add ¼ cup of water every hour or so. (Most packaged poultry comes with its weight and cooking time indicated.)

DRESSING

1 cup chicken livers and/or gizzards
1 cup onion, chopped
½ cup bell pepper, chopped
½ cup celery, chopped
2 cloves garlic, minced
1 medium pan baked cornbread, crumbled (see recipe on page 207)
4 Tbsp. parsley flakes
2 hard-cooked eggs, finely chopped
1 can chicken broth
1 can sliced mushrooms
1 can chicken gravy
½ tsp. salt
¼ tsp. black pepper
paprika
1 tsp. parsley flakes

1. Cook livers and gizzards in water to cover with the onion, bell pepper, celery, and garlic. Cut up giblets. Reserve broth.
2. In a large mixing bowl, combine cornbread, 4 Tbsp. parsley flakes, eggs, chicken broth, sliced mushrooms, chicken gravy, salt, pepper, and broth from cooked giblets. Place in greased baking dish.
3. Sprinkle paprika and 1 tsp. parsley flakes over top.
4. Bake at 350°F for 1–1½ hours.

GIBLET GRAVY

4 Tbsp. vegetable oil
4 Tbsp. self-rising flour
1 cup onion, chopped
½ cup green onions with tops, chopped
1 cup celery, chopped
1 cup bell pepper, chopped
1 can sliced mushrooms
1 cup cooked livers, gizzards, and broth
juices from baked hen or turkey
¼ cup parsley flakes
1 can sliced mushrooms
salt and pepper to taste

1. Heat vegetable oil. Add flour and stir constantly until dark brown.
2. Add remaining ingredients. Boil over medium heat for approximately 1–1½ hours. If the gravy is too thick, add more broth or water. If the gravy is too thin, slowly stir a paste of 2 Tbsp. flour mixed with ½ cup of water into boiling gravy.

Notes:

1. For all my gravy recipes, if the color of the gravy is not brown enough, I just add ½–1 Tbsp. Kitchen Bouquet.

2. In the event your gravy turns out too salty, don't worry. It's fixable. Just add a couple of teaspoonsful of instant dry mashed potatoes to the gravy. You may also have to add more liquid because the instant potatoes have a tendency to thicken whatever they're stirred into. This remedy will work no matter what kind of gravy you're cooking.

CHICKEN ON A CAN

Makes 4–6 servings

A friend of mine from Louisiana used this technique for years and finally convinced me to try it.

1 whole chicken
1 Tbsp. Worcestershire sauce
1 Tbsp. seasoned salt
1 tsp. black pepper
1 tsp. cayenne pepper
5 Tbsp. rosemary, divided
16 oz. can of beer

1. Using a sharp knife, cut slits in the chicken skin, spaced evenly over the whole chicken, and then rub with Worcestershire sauce.
2. Combine seasoned salt, black and cayenne peppers, and 1 tsp. of the rosemary. Rub over the chicken.
3. Cut the top off the beer can and remove one-third of the beer from the can. Put the remaining rosemary in the beer can and insert the open end of the can into the cavity of chicken.
4. Sit upright on a slow grill and let cook for about 2 hours or until done.
5. You can choose to brush your favorite barbecue sauce over the chicken as it roasts, or you can smoke it. The chicken will look like it is sitting up and visiting with you. It does not have to be turned, rotated, or moved until it is done. Just don't place it too close to the actual fire.

ZESTY BROASTED CHICKEN

Makes 6–10 servings

This is a very quick recipe to use when your preparation time is limited. It's also a good change from using barbecue sauce. A simple recipe, but it makes an excellent main course.

    1 or 2 whole chickens
       (depending on the number of people to be served)
    1 bottle of zesty Italian salad dressing

1. With a sharp knife, cut 2-inch slits, evenly spaced, over the chicken skin. Rub the Italian dressing over the chicken and place on grill.
2. You can do the chicken either on a rotisserie or in a smoker. If using a rotisserie, cook for 2 hours. If using a smoker, turn it often, and cook it for 40–45 minutes, watching carefully so as not to overdo it.

CRAWFISH ETOUFFEE

Makes 6 servings

1 onion, chopped
1 medium bell pepper, chopped
3 ribs celery, chopped
3 cloves garlic, minced
1 stick (¼ lb.) butter
half a can of tomatoes with chiles (mild or hot)
1 lb. crawfish tails
½–1 cup spicy tomato juice
salt to taste
red pepper to taste
black pepper to taste
hot sauce to taste
seasoned salt to taste
2 Tbsp. cornstarch

1. Sauté onion, bell pepper, celery, and garlic in butter for a few minutes.
2. Add tomatoes and cook for 10 minutes on a medium boil.
3. Add crawfish tails and enough spicy tomato juice to cover the mixture.
4. Season to taste with salt, peppers, hot sauce, and seasoned salt.
5. Cook on a medium to low heat for 30 minutes.
6. Combine cornstarch with a small amount of tap water. Dissolve well and then stir a small amount at a time into the mixture, until you get the thickness you want. Serve over rice.

Note:
Be careful with the amount of hot ingredients you add if you use the hot tomatoes and chiles. Be sure to taste before adding red pepper and hot sauce.

CRAWFISH PIE

Makes about 8 single-serving pies

1 onion, chopped
1 bell pepper, chopped
2 ribs celery, chopped
¾ cup butter
1½ lb. coarsely chopped, peeled crawfish tails
½ cup green onions and tops, finely chopped
½ cup parsley, minced
1½ tsp. salt
½ tsp. black pepper
⅛ tsp. red pepper
½ tsp. garlic powder
2 Tbsp. cornstarch
¼ cup water
1 piecrust recipe (see recipe on page 248)

1. Sauté onion, bell pepper, and celery in butter.
2. Add next seven ingredients. Simmer on low for 15 minutes.
3. Combine cornstarch and water until smooth. Stir into mixture until it reaches desired thickness. (The sauce should not be runny.)
4. Roll out crust to ⅛-inch thickness and cut two rounds for each pie. (You'll need to make sixteen rounds.) Use a saucer to measure your rounds.
5. Place ⅓ cup filling in the center of each of eight piecrust rounds. With your finger, moisten the outer edge of each filled round with a small amount of water. Put the top round of crust over the bottom crust with filling and seal with a fork.
6. Bake at 450°F until brown.

BAKED FLOUNDER WITH CRABMEAT STUFFING

Makes 6–8 servings

1 medium onion, chopped fine
1 shallot, chopped
2 cloves garlic, minced
2 Tbsp. celery, chopped
2 Tbsp. green bell pepper, chopped
4 Tbsp. butter or margarine, divided
1 cup crabmeat
1 tsp. salt
½ tsp. pepper
⅛ tsp. thyme
1 Tbsp. parsley, chopped
1 egg
¾ cup bread crumbs
3 or 4 large flounders

1. Sauté onion, shallot, garlic, celery, and green pepper in 2 Tbsp. of butter. Add crabmeat, salt, pepper, thyme, parsley, egg, and bread crumbs.
2. Melt the remaining 2 Tbsp. butter and brush over both sides of the fish.
3. Place a generous amount of stuffing in each fish.
4. Place fish in baking dish, not overlapping, dark side down.
5. Cover. Bake at 375°F for 30 minutes. Uncover during the last 10 minutes.

BAKED CATFISH

Makes 4 servings

2 fresh catfish halves
¼ tsp. red pepper
¼ tsp. paprika
¼ tsp. salt
¼ tsp. lemon pepper
¼ tsp. garlic pepper
½ cup minced onion
¼ cup minced celery
¼ cup minced bell pepper
¼ cup parsley flakes
3 cloves minced garlic
3 Tbsp. butter
half a lemon
1 tsp. Worcestershire sauce

1. Rinse fish halves and blot dry with paper towels.
2. Combine red pepper, paprika, salt, lemon pepper, and garlic pepper. Rub half the dry mix onto both sides of fish pieces.
3. Place both fish halves into a baking dish that has been greased with a little butter. Set aside.
4. Sauté onion, celery, bell pepper, parsley, and garlic in butter. Simmer on a low to medium heat for 3–4 minutes. Spread all over the top of both fish halves.
5. Mix remaining dry salt and peppers with juice from the lemon and Worcestershire sauce. Sprinkle over tops of stuffed fish.
6. Bake uncovered in 450°F oven for 20–30 minutes. Reduce oven heat to 300°F. Cover and bake for another 20 minutes or until fish is done. Baste with juices periodically. If the fish cooks dry, pour ¼ cup water around the outer edge of the baking dish. Do not pour over seasonings or fish.

FRIED FISH

Makes 4 servings

2 lb. fish fillets
½ cup buttermilk baking mix
½ cup yellow cornbread mix
1 egg, beaten
½ cup beer
vegetable oil

1. Rinse and cut fish into serving-size pieces. Set aside.
2. Sprinkle several spoonfuls of buttermilk baking mix over fish and toss to coat.
3. In a small bowl, combine remaining baking mix and cornbread mix with the beaten egg and beer until smooth.
4. Take one piece of a fish at a time and dip into batter. Let excess drip off.
5. Place into oil in preheated deep fryer and fry until golden brown on both sides.
6. Remove and drain on paper towels.

Note:
   For spicy-tasting fish, add ½ tsp. red pepper and ¼ tsp. garlic powder to the batter before dipping the fish.

BAKED SHRIMP

Makes 4 servings

2–3 lb. shrimp
¼ cup black pepper
1 cup Italian salad dressing
½ cup Worcestershire sauce
½ tsp. liquid concentrate shrimp and crab boil (available in the spice
    section of many grocery stores)
half stick (4 Tbsp.) butter, melted

1. Remove the heads from shrimp but leave the shells on. Rinse well with clear water. Place in a 13″ x 9″ glass baking dish.
2. Combine remaining ingredients and pour over shrimp. Refrigerate overnight.
3. Leave dish at room temperature for approximately one hour before baking. Bake at 400°F for 35–40 minutes.

Test doneness by removing one of the shrimp from the oven. When shrimp are done to your taste, remove from juices, peel and serve.

I serve a dish of the sauce alongside the shrimp for those who like to dip the shrimp and get that extra hot, zesty taste.

SKEWERED SHRIMP

Makes 2 servings

1 lb. shrimp, cleaned and shelled, with the tails left on
⅓ cup vegetable oil
¼ cup Sauternes
¼ cup soy sauce
1 clove garlic, crushed
¼ tsp. ground ginger
¼ tsp. paprika
¼ tsp. black pepper

1. Combine all ingredients and let shrimp marinate for 30 minutes.
2. Put shrimp on dampened bamboo skewers and grill for about 4 minutes on each side.

FRIED SHRIMP

Makes 4 servings

2–3 lb. shrimp
1 cup buttermilk baking mix, divided
½ tsp. salt
1 egg beaten
½ cup beer
pepper to taste
vegetable oil

1. Peel and rinse shrimp. Place approximately 4 Tbsp. baking mix in a small bowl. Roll shrimp in baking mix to coat. Set aside.
2. Mix remaining baking mix with the salt, egg, beer, and pepper. Mix until smooth. Dip each shrimp into the batter and let any excess drip off.
3. Have oil in deep fryer (or iron skillet) preheated. Fry shrimp until a golden brown. Remove and drain on paper towels.

OUTDOOR OYSTER ROAST

This recipe was given to me by a friend in Biloxi, Mississippi. I have written it down exactly as he gave it to me.

3 dozen oysters in their shells
½ lb. (2 sticks) butter, melted
½ cup pecans, finely chopped
2 tsp. tarragon wine vinegar

1. Prepare all ingredients because roasting is very quick.
2. Scrub oysters.
3. Balance a large iron skillet (I use one about 18 inches across) over the fire. Get the skillet spitting hot. Quickly lay oysters in skillet (hollow shell down) and cover quickly with a soaking wet burlap sack. This will give off a lot of steam.
4. In a separate skillet, heat the butter over the fire until it starts sizzling. Add pecans and stir until darkish brown—but don't let them burn.
5. Add vinegar to pecans. The sauce will bubble. Stir once and remove from the fire.
6. After about 4 or 5 minutes, lift the edge of the burlap sack and, with tongs, remove each oyster that has opened enough for a knife to be inserted. Continue to check the oysters that are still on the fire, lifting them off as they begin to open. Discard the flat top of the shell and serve oysters with pecans spooned over each.

COUNTRY SCRAPPLE

Makes 5–6 servings

Scrapple is an old Southern country standby recipe that many people our ages remember from their childhoods.

1 lb. loose pork sausage (not in casing)
2 cups yellow cornmeal
2 cups cold water
3½ cups, more or less, boiling water
1 tsp. salt
1 tsp. dried sage
1 tsp. cayenne pepper
flour
vegetable oil

1. Place sausage in a heavy pot with just enough water to cover. Boil over low heat for 30 minutes. Pour liquid from sausage into another pot and skim off fat.
2. Mix cornmeal with cold water. Blend with cooked sausage.
3. Add enough boiling water to the liquid drained from the sausage to make 1 quart. Add to sausage mixture.
4. Stir in salt, sage, and cayenne pepper. Stir until mixture thickens.
5. Cover and cook over low heat for 20 minutes, stirring frequently so it doesn't stick to the bottom of the stockpot. Pour into loaf pan. Chill for several hours.
6. When congealed, slice into 10 slices. Coat each with flour and brown in iron skillet in hot vegetable oil. Serve with scrambled eggs.

CHORIZO (MEXICAN SAUSAGE)

Makes 1 pound sausage

1 lb. deboned pork loin, uncooked
4 Tbsp. cider vinegar
2 Tbsp. chili powder
3 tsp. paprika
1 Tbsp. vegetable oil
½ tsp. sugar
1 tsp. dried oregano
1 tsp. ground cumin
1 tsp. salt
2 garlic cloves, crushed
sausage casings

1. Combine all ingredients in a food processor and pulse until well blended (or grind together in a food grinder).
2. Place the mixture in a container with a tight-fitting lid and refrigerate over night.
3. Stuff into casings that have been thoroughly washed.
4. To cook, put in heavy skillet with enough water to cover bottom of pan. Cook covered over low to medium heat for 30–35 minutes. Remove cover and brown.

BOUDAIN (CAJUN SAUSAGE)

Makes 2 pounds sausage

1 lb. lean ground pork
¼ lb. beef liver, ground
1 white onion, chopped
2 bunches green onions, chopped
1 Tbsp. cayenne pepper
1 Tbsp. black pepper
1 Tbsp. salt
1 Tbsp. MSG
1 cup cooked rice
½ cup dried parsley flakes
sausage casings

1. Place pork, liver, onions, peppers, salt, and MSG in pan. Add enough water just to cover. Boil for about 15 minutes. Drain.
2. Pour over rice and parsley. Stir and let sit for at least 10 minutes.
3. Stuff into casings that have been thoroughly washed.
4. To cook, put sausage links in heavy skillet with enough water to cover bottom of pan. Cook covered over low to medium heat for 30–35 minutes. Remove cover and continue cooking until meat browns.

TAMALES

Makes about 3 dozen tamales

The tamale is a popular Mexican dish. It can be made with various highly spiced fillings that are coated with a cornmeal dough, wrapped, and steamed.

This is a basic pork tamale wrapped with corn husks. You can also make chicken tamales much the same way. Many cooks serve sweet tamales, usually filled with fruit and wrapped in banana leaves.

In the South, tamales are traditionally served as dinner on Christmas Eve—but are wonderful anytime.

> 7 oz. bag corn husks
> 1 recipe masa dough (recipe following)
> 1 recipe (2 cups) red chili (recipe following)
> 1 recipe cooked pork butt (recipe following)

1. Cover the husks with boiling water (make sure they are all covered—you may have to put something heavy on top to weight them down) and leave to soak for about an hour. When the husks are softened, lightly blot them dry and flatten them on the counter with curling edges facing up.
2. Spread a scant ¼ cup of masa dough batter onto a husk in a 4-inch square, leaving at least a 1½-inch border along the pointy end of the husk and a ¾-inch border along the other sides.
3. On each husk, spoon about 2 Tbsp. of the pork-red chili filling down the center of the batter. Pick up the two long sides of the husk and bring them together so that the batter encloses the filling. Roll the flaps of the husk in the same direction around the tamale. If the husk is so small that the tamale doesn't seem well wrapped, add another husk. Fold up the empty, pointy end in a ½-inch section to close off the bottom. Secure it by loosely tying with a strip of husk torn from the extra husks.
4. To steam, place a metal rack in the bottom of a large stockpot. Keep the water level below the rack. Lay extra corn husks over the rack. Stand the tamales in the steamer with the open edge facing upward. After the bottom of the steamer is full, stack all other tamales on top. Place any extra husks on top of tamales, cover and steam for about 1 hour. Replenish boiling water if necessary during steaming time. The tamales are done when the husk peels away easily from the filling.

Dough (Masa)
    1 lb. shortening (lard)
    3 lb. fresh masa (very finely ground white cornmeal)
    chicken or pork stock, as needed
    2½ Tbsp. salt

1. Beat the lard with a mixer for about 10 minutes until it is very fluffy.
2. With the mixer still on medium speed, begin adding the masa a small amount at a time, stopping to scrape down the sides of the bowl as necessary. If the mixture becomes too stiff, add up to 1 cup lukewarm stock, a small amount at a time. When all the masa has been incorporated, the mixture should be the consistency of cream frosting.
3. Mix in ½ cup of the cooled red chili to color the batter evenly. Drop a teaspoon of the dough into a glass of water. If it floats, it's ready. If not, continue to beat. When it does float, the mixture is ready to be spread onto corn husks.

Pork Butt
    2½ lb. boneless pork butt
    1 whole head garlic, unpeeled
    1 tsp. black peppercorns
    4 large bay leaves
    1 tsp. salt, or to taste

1. Trim pork, leaving only a thin layer of fat. Place in large stockpot.
2. Slice the garlic crosswise in half. Add garlic, peppercorns, bay leaves, and salt to stockpot. Add enough cold water to cover by at least 2½ inches.
3. Bring just to a boil, quickly reduce heat to medium low, and let simmer, partially covered.
4. Skim froth from the top during the first 15 minutes of cooking. The meat should be well cooked in about 2 hours. Remove from stock and let cool to room temperature.
5. When cool, shred finely. Strain the stock. In a mixing bowl, combine the shredded pork with the red chili, reserving ½ cup chili to mix with the masa.

Continued on next page . . .

Red Chili

    6 oz. large, dried ancho chiles
    boiling water to cover
    2 tsp. dried oregano
    3 cloves garlic, peeled
    2 cups pork stock
    2 Tbsp. lard or vegetable oil
    1½ Tbsp. flour
    1 tsp. salt

1. Remove stems and seeds from chiles and rinse under cold running water. Pat dry. Place chiles (three or four at a time) in hot skillet and toast for 30–60 seconds, or just until the aroma is released. Be careful not to burn them. Place the toasted chiles in a bowl and cover with boiling water. Soak for about 10 minutes. Drain and discard the water.
2. Place chiles, oregano, garlic, and pork stock in blender and process to a smooth puree. Add more stock if it seems too thick. Work puree through a medium sieve into a bowl and discard any solids that remain.
3. Heat lard or oil in a medium saucepan over medium heat and add flour, stirring constantly until golden. Add strained chile puree and salt to the pan and reduce the heat to low. Cook over low heat, stirring often, until the flavor of the chiles has mellowed, about 10 minutes.

BARBECUE SAUCE I

Makes about 2 cups sauce

2 Tbsp. brown sugar
1 Tbsp. paprika
1 tsp. salt
1 tsp. dry mustard
¼ tsp. chili powder
¼ tsp. cayenne pepper
3 Tbsp. cooking oil
2 Tbsp. Worcestershire sauce
1 cup tomato juice
¼ cup ketchup
¼ cup vinegar
½ cup chopped onion

1. Combine ingredients.
2. Heat slowly for 15 minutes before using over meat.

BARBECUE SAUCE II

Makes about 2 cups sauce

½ cup prepared coffee
½ cup Worcestershire sauce
½ cup ketchup
¼ cup cider vinegar
¼ cup brown sugar
1 Tbsp. chili powder
1 tsp. salt
3 cloves garlic
1 Tbsp. liquid smoke
1 onion, chopped

1. Combine all ingredients in saucepan.
2. Bring to boil. Continue boiling for 20 minutes.

WHITE BARBECUE SAUCE

Makes about 1½ cups sauce

This sauce is very good to use with grilled chicken or fish.

  1 cup mayonnaise
  3 Tbsp. cider vinegar
  2 Tbsp. water
  1 tsp. salt
  ½ tsp. black pepper
  ½ tsp. cayenne pepper

Combine all ingredients in a bowl and whisk until smooth.

COCKTAIL SAUCE

Makes about 1 cup sauce

Use with shrimp, oysters, or fish.

½ cup chili sauce
½ cup ketchup
3 Tbsp. lemon juice
1 Tbsp. Worcestershire sauce
1 Tbsp. prepared horseradish
1 tsp. grated onion
½ tsp. hot pepper sauce
¼ tsp. salt
¼ tsp. pepper

Combine all ingredients.

One-Dish Meals

GROUND BEEF CASSEROLE

Makes 4–6 servings

1 lb. ground chuck
salt and pepper to taste
2 onions, sliced
1 can or 1 lb. pkg. frozen green peas
3–4 carrots, sliced
4 potatoes, sliced
2 cloves garlic, minced
1 can cream of celery soup
1½ cups crushed butter crackers

1. Brown ground chuck lightly. Sprinkle with salt and pepper. Place into a well-buttered casserole baking dish.
2. On top of the ground meat put a layer of onions, a layer of peas, a layer of carrots, and then a layer of potatoes.
3. Combine garlic and soup. Spread evenly over the top of vegetables.
4. Place crushed crackers on top.
5. Bake at 350°F for 1 hour, or until vegetables are tender.

PORK CHOP AND POTATO CASSEROLE

Makes 4 servings

2–3 white potatoes
1 large onion
4 center-cut or boneless pork chops
1 Tbsp. Worcestershire sauce
2 Tbsp. vegetable oil
¼ cup water
2 Tbsp. red cooking sherry
1 tsp. paprika
¼ cup parsley flakes
1 tsp. salt
1 tsp. black pepper

1. Peel potatoes and slice in thin round slices. Place in bowl with tap water to cover and set aside.
2. Peel the onions, slice in thin round slices, and set aside.
3. Wash the pork chops and blot dry. Rub the pork chops on both sides with Worcestershire sauce.
4. Preheat 2 Tbsp. oil in a large skillet. Pan-broil the pork chops on both sides until browned. Remove from skillet and set aside.
5. Add water and sherry to the skillet. Stir well to dislodge drippings. Set aside.
6. Place the pork chops in a greased oblong baking dish. Top with a layer of half the sliced, drained potatoes. Top with a layer of half the sliced onions. Repeat the potato and onion layer. Sprinkle with paprika, parsley, salt, and pepper. Drizzle with all liquids from the skillet. Cover with foil, sealing well.
7. Bake at 350°F for approximately 45 minutes, or until vegetables are tender. Serve with a spatula so that the pork chop is on the bottom and the potatoes and onions are on top. Spoon some of the liquid over each serving.

NO-BAKE GROUND BEEF SQUASH CASSEROLE

Makes 8–10 servings

This is my niece, Kim's, favorite. She lived with me from the age of eleven until she graduated from high school. I have seen her eat it cold from the fridge and enjoy it so much. I loved cooking it for her.

10 yellow crookneck squash
2–3 Tbsp. margarine
½ lb. ground chuck
1 cup chopped onion
1 cup chopped bell pepper
1 cup chopped celery
2–3 cloves garlic, chopped
½ cup diced cooked ham
half a can cream of mushroom soup
4 slices crisp toast, crushed
salt and pepper to taste

1. Clean, scrape and cut up squash. Place in a heavy pot with margarine. Cook over medium heat until the squash is tender, stirring constantly. Drain off any liquid that accumulated.
2. In a frying pan, simmer the ground chuck just until cooked, but not browned. Combine the ground chuck, the squash, and all other ingredients except the toast crumbs, salt, and pepper. Simmer on a very low heat for approximately 45 minutes. The consistency should be very thick.
3. Season with salt and peppers. Pour into a casserole dish. Top with the toast crumbs and serve.

***Note*:**
   I usually add ½ cup shredded cheddar cheese to the mixture right before pouring it into the dish. That's optional, but I think the cheese gives the dish a better texture and taste.

STUFFED BAKED SQUASH

Makes 6 servings

4 medium yellow squash
1 cup lean ground meat
1 cup onion, chopped
½ cup bell pepper, chopped
½ cup celery, chopped
1 clove garlic, minced
1 Tbsp. parsley flakes
1 small can chopped mushrooms
1 egg
½ cup milk
1 Tbsp. self-rising flour
salt and pepper to taste
½ cup cheddar cheese, grated

1. Cut off stems and ends of squash. Scrape and rinse well. Slice lengthwise into halves. Place in water and boil until tender. Remove from water and let cool. When cooled enough to handle, scoop out the center of each and set aside.
2. In a separate saucepan, cook the ground beef over medium heat.
3. Add onion, bell pepper, celery, garlic, parsley, and mushrooms. Sauté for approximately 10 minutes.
4. In a small bowl, mix egg, milk, and flour until smooth.
5. Combine squash scooped from shells, egg mixture, and meat mixture.
6. Salt and pepper to taste. Fill each squash shell to capacity.
7. Top with shredded cheese.
8. Bake at 350°F for approximately 10 minutes.

TAMALE BEEF SQUARES

Makes 9 squares

1 lb. ground beef
1 large onion, chopped
¼ cup water
1 Tbsp. chili powder
½ cup mild green chiles, drained
½ tsp. garlic powder
½ tsp. salt
14½ oz. can diced tomatoes, drained
⅔ cup frozen corn
8 oz. pkg. cornbread mix
⅓ cup milk (skim works fine)
1 egg
1 Tbsp. vegetable oil
1 cup cheddar cheese, grated

1. In a medium skillet, cook crumbled ground meat, onion, and water over medium heat for 5–7 minutes, stirring occasionally.
2. Add chili powder, drained chiles, garlic powder, and salt. Cook uncovered 8–10 minutes over medium heat, stirring often until the meat is browned, stirring to break meat into small pieces.
3. Stir tomatoes and corn into skillet. Remove from heat.
4. In a medium bowl, combine cornbread mix, milk, egg, and vegetable oil. Stir until evenly blended.
5. Spread cornbread mixture over bottom of greased baking pan. Spread meat mixture over the cornbread layer. Sprinkle with cheese.
6. Bake at 350°F for 30 minutes or until cheese is melted and slightly bubbly.

CHICKEN BROCCOLI CASSEROLE

Makes 6 servings

3 chicken breasts
½ cup onion, chopped
½ cup bell pepper, chopped
¼ cup celery, chopped
2 cloves garlic, minced
2 tsp. parsley flakes
salt and pepper to taste
10 oz. pkg. frozen chopped broccoli, cooked
1 cup dry rice, cooked
1 can cream of mushroom soup
1 can cream of chicken soup
1 can sliced water chestnuts
1 can mushroom stems and pieces
1 small jar cheese spread
¼ cup shredded cheddar cheese
¼ cup shredded mozzarella cheese
paprika
parsley flakes

1. In large saucepan cover chicken breasts with water to cover and bring to boil.
2. Add onion, bell pepper, celery, garlic, parsley, salt, and pepper. Simmer for approximately 35 minutes on medium heat. Remove chicken from broth, debone, and cut into small pieces. Return chicken to broth. Set aside.
3. Combine broccoli, rice, chicken and broth, condensed soups, water chestnuts, mushrooms, and cheese spread.
4. Pour into a greased 13" x 9" pan. Top with shredded cheeses. Sprinkle a small amount of paprika and a small amount of parsley flakes on top of cheese.
5. Bake at 350°F for 45 minutes. The finished casserole should be thick and creamy.

CHICKEN SPAGHETTI

Makes 6–8 servings

1 chicken or 3 chicken breasts
3 cups water
1 cup onion, chopped
1 cup bell pepper, chopped
1 cup celery, chopped
2 cloves garlic, minced
¼ cup parsley, chopped
1 can sliced mushrooms
1 can cream of mushroom soup
1 can cream of celery soup
¼ tsp. lemon pepper
salt and pepper to taste
10–12 oz. dry spaghetti

1. Boil chicken in water until tender. Remove chicken from broth and debone. Cut into small pieces and set aside. Return broth to stove and bring to a medium boil.
2. Add remaining ingredients except spaghetti. Cook over medium heat for 30–40 minutes.
3. Cook spaghetti according to pkg. directions. Drain well and add to chicken mixture. Turn burner as low as you can and let stand until ready to serve.

Note:

You may serve the chicken mixture on top of spaghetti instead of mixed together. You can also use any pasta that you wish.

LOUISIANA DIRTY RICE

Makes 6–8 servings

1 lb. chicken livers
½ lb. lean ground beef
1 large onion, chopped
1 green pepper, chopped
2 ribs celery, chopped
3 green onions, chopped
2 tsp. salt
¼ tsp. cayenne pepper
¼ tsp. thyme
1 bay leaf
2 cups chicken broth
2 cups cooked rice

1. Cover chicken livers in lightly salted water and bring to boil. Cook until tender. Cool, grind, and set aside. Reserve cooking water.
2. In large saucepan, cook ground beef over medium heat with chopped onion, pepper, celery, and green onions, stirring often.
3. Add salt, cayenne, thyme, bay leaf, and chicken broth. Simmer for 30 minutes on low heat.
4. Add chicken livers just before removing from heat. Mix well.
5. Remove bay leaf. Stir in ½ cup reserved chicken liver cooking water.
6. Stir in freshly steamed rice. Cover tightly and let stand for 15 minutes before serving.

CHICKEN POT PIE

Makes one 9-inch pie

2 large chicken breasts
2 cups water
1 medium onion, chopped
½ cup bell pepper, chopped
½ cup celery, chopped
2 cloves garlic, minced
4 green onions with tops, chopped
½ cup carrots, cubed
1 large potato
½ cup small green peas
1 can cream of mushroom soup
1 cup chicken gravy
salt and pepper to taste
¼ cup parsley, chopped
double piecrust, unbaked (see recipe on page 248)
margarine, melted
parsley flakes
paprika

1. Boil chicken breasts in water for approximately one hour or until tender. Remove from broth, debone and cut into pieces. Add chicken back to broth.
2. Stir in next thirteen ingredients. Cook on medium heat for approximately 20 minutes. Set aside.
3. Prebake bottom piecrust 5–6 minutes in a 350°F oven. Remove from oven.
4. Spoon in chicken mixture. Top with unbaked piecrust. Brush with margarine. Sprinkle with parsley flakes and paprika.
5. Bake in a 350°F oven for about 35 minutes or until top is golden brown.

CHICKEN AND BISCUIT CASSEROLE

Makes 6 servings

3½ cups water
2 chicken breasts
½ cup onion, chopped
¼ cup celery, chopped
2 cloves garlic, minced
salt and pepper to taste
½ cup whole or low-fat milk
½ cup evaporated milk
3 Tbsp. flour
1 can butterflake biscuits

1. Combine water, chicken, onions, celery, garlic, salt, and pepper. Bring to a boil, adding water as needed to keep chicken just covered. Simmer for approximately 30 minutes, or until chicken is tender. Remove chicken and set broth aside. Debone chicken and cut into bite-sized pieces.
2. In a small bowl, mix milks and flour, dissolving flour well. Add to broth mixture and return to stove. Stir frequently over low heat until broth thickens. Add chicken back to mixture and then pour into greased casserole.
3. Pull biscuits apart into individual thin slices and place on top of mixture. (Use all the biscuit flakes.)
4. Bake at 400°F for 10–15 minutes or until biscuit flakes are an even golden brown.

Note:
You can also add peas and carrots to the chicken and vegetables before boiling in Step 1.

KING RANCH CHICKEN

Makes 6–8 servings

3–4 lb. chicken
water to cover chicken
2 onions, chopped
2 ribs celery, chopped
1 large green pepper, chopped
salt and pepper to taste
1 can cream of chicken soup
1 can cream of mushroom soup
10 oz. grated cheddar cheese, divided
12 corn tortillas
chili powder
garlic salt
10 oz. can tomatoes with green chiles

1. Combine chicken, water, onion, celery, bell pepper, salt, and pepper. Boil until chicken is tender. Remove chicken from broth and cut into bite-size pieces. Reserve stock.
2. Combine soups and grated cheese (reserve ¼ cup cheese to sprinkle on top).
3. Just before assembling casserole, soak tortillas in boiling chicken stock until softened.
4. In a greased 9″ x 13″ pan, layer half the following ingredients in this order: tortillas, chicken, cooked vegetables (sprinkle to taste with chili powder and garlic salt), and soup mixture. Repeat the layers.
5. Cover the casserole with undrained tomatoes and chiles. Sprinkle remaining cheese over top. Juices in the casserole should be about half the depth of the dish. If not, add a little more stock.
6. Bake uncovered at 375°F for 30 minutes.

Note:
   This dish is better if made one day ahead and refrigerated so the flavors can blend.

CHILE CHICKEN RELLENOS PIE

Makes 6–8 servings

2 cans whole green chiles
1 lb. Monterey Jack cheese, sliced
1 lb. cheddar cheese, sliced
4 tsp. whole wheat flour
1 cup evaporated milk
1 cup sour cream
4 eggs
1 cup cooked chicken, diced
2 cups mild salsa

1. Cut chiles open and line a greased 9″ x 13″ baking dish with them.
2. Layer both cheeses evenly over chiles.
3. Add any remaining chiles over the cheese layer.
4. Mix flour with a small amount of milk. Using a wire whisk, make a smooth paste. Mix in remaining milk and sour cream.
5. Beat in eggs, one at a time.
6. Add diced chicken. Pour this mixture over chiles and cheese.
7. Bake at 350°F for 30 minutes.
8. Pour salsa over top and bake an additional 15 minutes.

SHRIMP AND ARTICHOKE CASSEROLE

Makes 4–6 servings

4 oz. can artichoke hearts
1 lb. cooked shrimp
¼ lb. sliced mushrooms
4 Tbsp. butter, divided
2 Tbsp. flour
1½ cups milk
1 Tbsp. Worcestershire sauce
½ tsp. salt
½ tsp. white pepper
¼ cup dry sherry
¼ cup grated Parmesan cheese
dash paprika
chopped parsley

1. Drain artichoke hearts and arrange in a buttered baking dish.
2. Spread cooked shrimp over layer of artichokes.
3. Sauté sliced mushrooms in 2 Tbsp. butter. Remove with a slotted spoon and add to the baking dish.
4. Add remaining butter to skillet and sprinkle with flour. Stir well and add milk to make a cream sauce.
5. Add seasonings, sherry, and Parmesan to the cream sauce. Pour over contents of baking dish.
6. Sprinkle top with paprika.
7. Bake for 20 minutes in a 350°F oven. Cover dish with finely chopped parsley.

FISH COURT BOUILLON

Makes 6–8 servings

This is pronounced "cu'b'ahn" and is my husband's favorite meal. This is his mother's recipe.

⅓ cup vegetable oil
3 Tbsp. self-rising flour
1 onion, chopped
2 ribs celery, chopped
1 clove garlic, minced
1 bell pepper, cut into thin long slices
14½ oz. can tomatoes, mashed
½ cup tomato sauce
2 cups water
2 bay leaves
1 whole clove allspice
1½–2 lb. fresh fish, cut into small pieces
2 green onions, tops and bottoms chopped
2 Tbsp. parsley flakes
2 lemon slices
salt to taste
black pepper to taste
red pepper to taste
cooked rice

1. Make a roux by heating oil in heavy pot. Add flour and stir until a dark brown.
2. Add onion, celery, garlic, and half the bell pepper. Cook for about 5 minutes.
3. Add mashed tomatoes, tomato sauce, and water. Cook for 45 minutes.
4. Add bay leaves and allspice. Add more water if needed.
5. Add fish and cook for 15–20 minutes or until the fish is done.
6. Add remaining bell pepper strips, green onions, and parsley. Add lemon. Season with salt, black pepper, and red pepper. Cook for 10 minutes more.
7. Remove bay leaves and clove of allspice, and serve court bouillon over cooked rice.

CAJUN RICE JAMBALAYA

Makes 6 servings

1 pint chicken livers
6–8 inches smoked pork sausage
5 Tbsp. vegetable oil
5 Tbsp. self-rising flour
1 onion, chopped
2 cloves garlic, minced
2 Tbsp. dried parsley flakes
1 can chicken broth, *optional*
salt and pepper to taste
2 cups cooked rice

1. Boil chicken livers in lightly salted water for 15 minutes. Chop finely. Reserve water.
2. Brown sausage over low heat for about 15 minutes and cube.
3. Heat vegetable oil in heavy pot. Add flour, stirring constantly until dark brown in color, but being careful not to burn it. If the flour seems too dry, add about ½ Tbsp. oil.
4. Add onion, garlic, parsley, and broth from boiled livers. Cook until broth reaches a gravy consistency. If too thick, add one can chicken broth.
5. Add the finely chopped chicken livers and cubed sausage.
6. Salt and pepper to taste.
7. Cook for approximately 30 minutes. Turn heat to low and add the precooked rice. Stir well and let stand until ready to serve.

The jambalaya should stand in a mound when served. If the mixture is too thin, add a little more rice. If too thick, add a little more chicken broth.

Note:
I like this very hot so I add two seeded and chopped jalapeño peppers when I add the onions.

STUFFED CABBAGE

Makes about 6 servings

1 head cabbage
¾ lb. ground beef
1 small onion, finely chopped
1 clove garlic, minced
1 cup cooked rice
1 egg
1 tsp. oregano
8 oz. can tomato sauce, divided
salt and pepper to taste
½ cup olive oil
1 bay leaf, crushed
2 cups beef broth
½ cup white wine
water

1. Remove core of cabbage. Parboil cabbage for 5 minutes in lightly salted water. Remove from water and drain. Separate cabbage leaves. Chop the small inside leaves and line a Dutch oven with them.
2. Combine ground beef, chopped onion, garlic, rice, egg, oregano, 2 Tbsp. tomato sauce, salt, and pepper. Mix well.
3. Place 1 Tbsp. of stuffing on each of the larger cabbage leaves. Fold ends of leaves over stuffing, then roll up leaves. Place packets in layers in the Dutch oven.
4. Sprinkle each layer with olive oil, tomato sauce, crushed bay leaf, salt, and pepper before adding the next layer. Continue layering until all stuffed cabbage leaves have been used.
5. Combine remaining tomato sauce, beef broth, wine, and enough water to cover cabbage leaves and pour over the stuffed leaves.
6. Place a heavy plate on top of the cabbage rolls. Simmer over low heat for 1 hour. Serve with sauce poured over the rolls.

Breads

STUFFED CORNBREAD

Makes 6 servings

1 lb. ground beef
1 small onion
salt to taste
black pepper to taste
1 small can chopped green chiles
1 cup yellow cornmeal
1 cup flour
¾ tsp. baking soda
2 tsp. baking powder
½ tsp. salt
⅓ cup vegetable oil
2 eggs
1 cup buttermilk
1 small can creamed corn
1¼ cups grated cheddar cheese

1. Brown ground beef and onion in saucepan.
2. Add salt and black pepper to taste.
3. Stir in chiles.
4. In a medium bowl, mix together cornmeal, flour, baking soda, baking powder, ½ tsp. salt, oil, eggs, and buttermilk. Stir in the corn. Mix well.
5. Pour a small amount of oil into a 9-inch, oven-proof skillet. Spoon half the cornbread mixture into the skillet. Cover with the meat mixture. Sprinkle grated cheese over meat and top with remaining cornbread mixture.
6. Bake at 400°F for 30 minutes.

ANADAMA BREAD

Makes 2 loaves

Legend has it that a farmer had a lazy wife named Anna, who always served him cornmeal mush for dinner. He finally decided to try his own hand at cooking, and, by adding extra ingredients to the mush, he made a bread—thus "Anna damn 'er" bread.

½ cup yellow cornmeal
2 cups boiling water
2 Tbsp. butter
½ cup molasses
1 tsp. salt
1 pkg. active dry yeast
5 cups flour

1. Stir cornmeal slowly into water just as it begins to boil. Boil for 5 minutes, stirring constantly.
2. Add butter, molasses, and salt. Cool.
3. When mixture is lukewarm, add softened yeast and enough flour to make a stiff dough. Knead well and set in a warm place to rise until double in bulk.
4. Shape into two loaves and place in buttered loaf pans. Let rise again.
5. Bake at 350°F for about 1 hour.

SQUASH MUFFINS

Makes 18 muffins

8 cups sliced yellow crookneck squash (about 2 lb.), unpeeled
½ cup milk
⅓ cup margarine, melted
2 eggs, lightly beaten
3 cups flour
2 Tbsp. sugar
1 Tbsp. baking powder
¾ tsp. salt

1. In a large saucepan, combine squash with just enough lightly salted water to cover and bring to a boil. Cover, reduce heat, and simmer for 30 minutes or until tender. Drain well. Mash squash and drain through a strainer. Discard liquid.
2. Combine squash, milk, margarine, and eggs. Stir well and set aside.
3. Combine flour, sugar, baking powder, and salt. Make a well in the center of the dry mixture.
4. Add squash mixture to the dry ingredients, stirring just until dry ingredients are moistened.
5. Divide batter evenly among eighteen muffin tin molds coated with vegetable cooking spray.
6. Bake at 375°F for 20 minutes. Remove from pan and let cool on wire rack.

BEATEN BISCUITS

Makes 8–10 biscuits

Years ago cooks were told to beat this biscuit dough (usually with a metal pestle) from three hundred to five hundred licks. Three hundred was okay for everyday eating, but for "company," five hundred times was considered better.

2 cups flour
½ tsp. salt
½ cup shortening
⅓ cup water

1. Combine flour and salt.
2. Cut in shortening until mixture resembles coarse meal.
3. Gradually add water, mixing with a fork until a very stiff dough is formed.
4. Place dough on a floured surface and beat with a very heavy rolling pin, turning dough often. After about 20 minutes of firm beating, tiny blisters will appear on the surface.
5. Roll dough out to about ½-inch thickness and cut with biscuit cutter.
6. Place on greased baking sheet so they don't touch, and prick each biscuit with a fork.
7. Bake at 350°F for about 20 minutes or until they just begin to brown.

BUTTERMILK BISCUITS

Makes 8–10 biscuits

2½ cups self-rising flour
⅓ cup butter-flavored shortening
⅔ cup buttermilk

1. Sift flour into large mixing bowl.
2. Make a well in the center with your hand. Place shortening into this indentation.
3. Pour buttermilk into the well and mix with your hand, squeezing flour, shortening, and milk together. Stay in the center of the bowl while mixing. Slowly pull flour into the mixture from the sides of the bowl.
4. When the dough is of a consistency that can be rolled, pinch dough off in amounts the size of an egg. Roll each into a small ball in your hand. Place in a well-greased baking pan. Press the tops of biscuits with your hand to ½-inch thickness.
5. Bake at 450°F until golden brown.

BEER BISCUITS

Makes about 2 dozen biscuits

4 cups buttermilk baking mix
4 oz. sour cream
1 cup beer
1 stick (¼ lb.) butter or margarine, melted

1. Combine baking mix, sour cream, and beer. Mix well.
2. Roll by hand into balls about the size of an egg.
3. Pour half the melted butter into a baking pan. Place dough balls in the buttered pan and press each one down to about ½-inch thickness. Pour other half of melted butter over biscuits.
4. Bake at 375°F for 20 minutes or until golden brown

Note:

For those who do not want the beer, you can substitute 1 cup of club soda.

CHEESE SAUSAGE BISCUITS

Makes 12–15 biscuits

1 lb. loose pork sausage
3 cups buttermilk baking mix
10 oz. sharp cheese, grated

1. Crumble sausage into frying pan over medium heat. Stir frequently and cook just until the meat loses its pink color. Remove from stove and let cool.
2. Place baking mix in large bowl. Add cheese, sausage, and sausage drippings. Mix until you are able to form a ball with the dough.
3. Pinch off the dough and roll into 1–2½-inch balls. Place balls of dough in a slightly greased baking pan. Press down with a fork or with your hand until they are ½ inch high.
4. Bake at 350°F until they are golden brown. Bake only what you need. Freeze the remainder of the mixed dough until you're ready to use it.

Note:

Do not fry the sausage completely. You only want it partially cooked since it will cook further as the biscuits bake.

FRIED SQUARE BISCUITS

Makes 10–15 biscuits

I love these plain when I serve spaghetti and meatballs. They are also good with any kind of stew.

1½ cups self-rising flour
1 Tbsp. butter-flavored shortening
¾ cup milk
vegetable oil

1. Place flour into a large mixing bowl. Form a well in the center of the flour with your hand.
2. Place shortening in the flour and slowly add the milk. Mix with your hands as you would with any pan biscuits. Work in flour until you have a ball of dough that stays firm.
3. Roll out on a floured surface and cut into strips about 1" x 2" and about ¼ inch thick.
4. Drop into preheated oil in a deep fryer. Fry until golden brown on both sides. This takes only a few minutes. Remove from oil and drain on paper towels.

   These puff up to twice their original size and are crispy on the inside.

Optional:

Sprinkle a little powdered sugar on the biscuit tops while they are hot, or mix ½ cup powdered sugar with a tablespoon of your favorite jelly and drizzle over the tops.

BONANZA BREAD

Makes 2 loaves

This is a tasty, nutritious bread that is good toasted for breakfast.

1 cup sifted all-purpose flour
1 cup whole wheat flour
½ tsp. salt
½ tsp. baking soda
2 tsp. baking powder
⅔ cup nonfat dry milk powder
⅓ cup wheat germ
½ cup firmly packed brown sugar
¼ cup chopped walnuts
½ cup chopped dry roasted peanuts
½ cup raisins
3 eggs
¼ cup oil
½ cup molasses
¾ cup orange juice
2 medium-sized bananas, mashed
⅓ cup chopped dried apricots

1. Combine flours, salt, baking soda, baking powder, dry milk, wheat germ, brown sugar, nuts, and raisins in a large bowl. Blend thoroughly.
2. Whirl eggs in blender until foamy. Add oil, molasses, orange juice, and bananas, whirling after each addition.
3. Add apricots and whirl just to chop coarsely.
4. Pour mixture into bowl with dry ingredients. Stir just until all flour is moistened. Pour into two greased loaf pans.
5. Bake at 325°F for 1 hour until center is firm when pressed lightly. Cool slightly before removing from pan.

CHOICE MUFFINS

Makes 12 muffins

2 cups all-purpose flour
2¼ tsp. baking powder
1 tsp. salt
½ cup sugar
1 egg, beaten
1 cup milk
2 Tbsp. vegetable oil

1. Sift together the flour, baking powder, salt, and sugar. Set aside.
2. Combine egg, milk, and oil. Beat vigorously. Stir into flour mixture. Mix well. Batter will have a slightly lumpy appearance.
3. Place by spoonfuls into paper baking cups in the muffin tin.
4. Bake at 400°F for about 20 minutes.

Variations:
1. Place one spoonful of batter into each muffin cup. Then place a teaspoon of grape (or other flavor) jelly over top the batter in each cup. Cover each with another spoonful of batter. Bake as directed.
2. Add drained blueberries into batter before spooning into baking cups. Use your imagination. You can add nuts, cherries, or any other fruit.
3. You can also ice the baked muffins with your favorite icing.

CORNBREAD

Makes 6–8 servings

Cornbread was a staple in most early Southern homes. Cornbread was made daily, or more often, in the old cast-iron skillet. These cast-iron skillets at one time were placed on a cast-iron base with legs so the bread would cook above the hot coals in the hearth. The pans were called spiders because with the legs on their base they looked somewhat like a spider. Cornbread was often called "spider bread."

1 egg
¼ cup vegetable oil or melted butter
1 cup buttermilk
1 cup yellow self-rising cornmeal
1 Tbsp. self-rising flour

1. Combine egg, oil, and buttermilk.
2. Combine dry ingredients and add to egg mixture. Mix well.
3. Grease a skillet, cornstick pan, or muffin tin. If you're using a skillet, pour in all the batter. If you're using a stick pan or muffin tins, make them only about half full.
4. Bake at 425°F for 15–20 minutes or until golden brown. If you're baking in a skillet, test the center with a toothpick to be sure the bread is thoroughly baked.

MEXICAN CORNBREAD

Makes 6–8 slices

2 eggs
⅔ cup vegetable oil
1 cup sour cream
1 cup yellow cornmeal
1 cup yellow creamed corn
1 Tbsp. baking powder
1½ tsp. salt
4 jalapeño peppers, seeded and finely chopped
1 cup grated sharp cheddar cheese, divided

1. Combine eggs, oil, sour cream, cornmeal, corn, baking powder, and salt.
2. Add peppers and half the cheese.
3. Spread in a well-greased baking pan or iron skillet.
4. Cover with the remaining cheese.
5. Bake at 400°F for about 30 minutes.

Note:

   This recipe is great for hush puppies, too. Just add more cornmeal, a little at a time, until you have a much thicker batter. Drop by spoonfuls into hot oil (deep enough to cover the puppies) and fry on both sides until golden brown.

HUSH PUPPIES

On fishing and hunting trips, hound dogs that accompanied their masters would begin barking when they smelled the aroma of dinner cooking on the open fire. In order to quiet the dogs, the men would drop pieces of cornmeal batter into hot fat to fry, then toss them to the hounds and say, "Hush, Puppy." Thus began the Southern tradition of fried fish and hush puppies.

2 cups fine cornmeal
2 Tbsp. baking powder
1 tsp. salt
1¼ cups milk
½ cup water
½ cup finely chopped onions

1. Sift together cornmeal, baking powder, and salt.
2. Combine milk and water, and stir into cornmeal mixture until well blended.
3. Stir in onions.
4. Add more cornmeal if needed to make a stiff dough.
5. Drop by tablespoonfuls into deep hot fat until browned on all sides.
6. Serve hot with fried fish.

JOHNNY CAKE

Makes 2 flat loaves

This is a basic recipe from early Southern homes which was given many names, indicating something about its adaptability—Johnny cake, ash cake, hoe cake, corn dodgers, and corn pone.

It is thought to have originally been called "journey cake" because it kept so well on trips. Through time, the name became "Johnny" cake. Others say it was named after the Southern soldier, Johnny Rebs.

The batter was sometimes placed on the blade of hoes or shovels and baked in hot wood ashes on an outdoor fire or in fireplaces. These loaves were called "hoe cakes."

The loaves were often cooked directly on the open hearth with a covering of hot ashes. Then it was called "ash bread." Loaves were sometimes protected from the ashes by a covering of cabbage leaves, but at other times they were baked right among the ashes. It is said that a good cook could serve ash bread with no evidence of ash showing on the loaf.

The bread was often simply known as "corn dodgers" or "corn pone" because of its basic ingredient.

2 cups cornmeal
1 tsp. salt
3 cups boiling water
3 Tbsp. shortening

1. Combine cornmeal and salt.
2. Pour boiling water over dry mixture.
3. Add shortening. Beat until smooth.
4. Spread in 2 greased 8-inch baking pans.
5. Bake at 350°F for about 40 minutes or until crisp.

LOUISIANA LOST BREAD

Makes 4 servings

1 egg
⅛ tsp. salt
1 Tbsp. sugar
¼ cup milk
¼ tsp. vanilla
4 slices of bread

1. Beat egg.
2. Add salt, sugar, milk, and vanilla.
3. Pour into a shallow dish. One-by-one, dip bread slices into egg-milk mixture and let each slice absorb as much liquid as possible on both sides.
4. Place slices in a greased baking pan.
5. Bake at 400°F until bread is dry and brown.
6. Serve with butter and honey or dust with powdered sugar.

MOLASSES BREAD

Makes 1 loaf

1 pkg. dry yeast
¼ cup molasses
1¼ cups warm water
2 Tbsp. butter or margarine, melted
3½ cups all-purpose flour, divided
¾ cup cornmeal
2 tsp. salt
cooking spray

1. Dissolve yeast and molasses in warm water and let stand for 5 minutes. Add melted butter or margarine.
2. Add 3 cups flour, cornmeal, and salt to yeast mixture. Stir until blended.
3. On a lightly floured surface, knead dough for about 8 minutes until smooth and elastic, adding remaining flour as needed. Place in a bowl coated with cooking spray, turning to coat top. Cover and let rise in a warm place (85°F) for one hour or until doubled in size.
4. Punch dough down. Roll into a 14" x 7" rectangle on a floured surface. Roll up rectangle tightly, starting with a short edge, pressing firmly to eliminate air pockets. Pinch seam and ends to seal.
5. Place roll, seam side down, in a greased 9" x 5" loaf pan.
6. Cover and let rise one hour or until doubled in size.
7. Bake at 350°F for 45 minutes, or until loaf sounds hollow when tapped.

CINNAMON POTATO ROLLS

Makes 18 rolls

¾ cup sugar
¾ cup hot mashed potatoes
1½ cups warm water (110°–115°F)
2 pkg. active dry yeast
½ cup butter or margarine, softened
2 eggs
2 tsp. salt
6½ cups all-purpose flour

Filling:
    1⅓ cups packed brown sugar
    1 tsp. ground cinnamon
    3 Tbsp. butter or margarine, softened

Powdered Sugar Icing:
    powdered sugar
    vanilla
    milk

1. In a large mixing bowl, combine sugar and mashed potatoes.
2. Add water and yeast. Mix well. Cover and let rise in a warm place for 1 hour.
3. Meanwhile, combine filling ingredients and set aside.
4. Stir dough down. Mix in butter, eggs, and salt. Gradually stir in flour.
5. Turn out onto a lightly floured surface and knead until smooth and elastic, about 8 minutes.
6. Divide dough in half. On a floured surface, roll each portion into a 12-inch square.
7. Divide filling and spread over each square to within 1 inch of the edges. Roll up each square, jelly-roll style.
8. Cut each roll into nine slices. Place in a greased 9″ x 9″ baking pan. Cover and let rise in a warm place until doubled in size, about 1 hour.
9. Bake at 350°F for 35–40 minutes, or until golden.
10. Drizzle with icing made by mixing powdered sugar and a drop or two of vanilla with enough milk to be of a thin consistency.

HONEY WHEAT BREAD

Makes 8 small loaves

2 cups all-purpose flour (or bread flour)
1⅔ cups wheat flour
1 Tbsp. cocoa powder
1 Tbsp. granulated sugar
2 tsp. instant coffee powder
1 tsp. salt
1½ cups warm water
2 Tbsp. butter, softened
½ cup honey
1 pkg. (or 2¼ tsp.) dry yeast
cornmeal

1. Combine flours, cocoa powder, sugar, dry coffee, and salt in a large bowl. Make a well in the middle of the dry mixture.
2. Pour warm water into well. Add butter, honey, and yeast. Mix the ingredients well. When you can handle the dough, begin to combine it by hand, kneading the dough thoroughly for at least 10 minutes, until it is very smooth. Place the dough in a greased bowl, cover, and allow to rise in a warm place for 1 hour.
3. When the dough has risen to about double its original size, punch down and divide into eight even portions. Form the eight portions into tubular-shaped loaves, about 8 inches long and 2 inches wide.
4. Sprinkle the entire surface of the loaves with cornmeal and place them on greased cookie sheets. Cover the loaves loosely and let the dough rise in a warm place again for 1 hour.
5. Bake at 350°F for 20–25 minutes.

SOURDOUGH STARTER

1 pkg. dry yeast
2½ cups warm water, divided
2 cups all-purpose flour
1 Tbsp. sugar

1. Soften yeast in ½ cup warm water.
2. Stir in flour, remaining warm water, and sugar. Beat until smooth.
3. Cover and let stand at room temperature for 5–10 days or until bubbly. Stir two or three times daily.
4. Refrigerate until ready to use. When needed, allow starter to reach room temperature before mixing into bread dough.
5. After using a portion of the starter, renew it by adding ¾ cup flour, ¾ cup water and 1 tsp. sugar to remaining starter. If not used in 10 days, add 1 tsp. sugar to keep the starter going. Many people put a quartered raw potato into their starter for added leavening.

Note:

Some Southern cooks made bread using only sourdough starter, flour, and water. It is also said that the sourdough starter was so valuable for leavening that some cooks kept it at the foots of their beds in order to keep it warm at night.

SOURDOUGH ROLLS

Makes about 1½ dozen rolls

1 pkg. yeast
½ cup warm water
⅓ cup sugar
1 egg

1 tsp. salt
⅓ cup vegetable oil
1½ cups sourdough starter
3½ cups flour

1. Dissolve yeast in warm water.
2. Add sugar, egg, salt, oil, sourdough starter, and flour. Mix well.
3. Let rise for about 2 hours. Punch down and shape into rolls.
4. Bake with sides touching in greased baking pan at 375°F for 20 minutes.

ORANGE CINNAMON SOURDOUGH ROLLS

Makes 12 rolls

2 cups self-rising flour
¾ cup sourdough starter
⅔ cup buttermilk
2 Tbsp. butter or margarine,
    melted

½ cup sugar
1 Tbsp. orange peel, finely
    shredded
2 tsp. ground cinnamon
1 Tbsp. melted butter

Icing:
    1 cup powdered sugar, sifted
    1 tsp. vanilla
    2 Tbsp. milk

1. Combine flour, sourdough starter, and buttermilk. Turn onto floured surface and knead fifteen times.
2. Roll to a 12-inch square.
3. Brush with 2 Tbsp. melted butter.
4. Combine sugar, orange peel, and cinnamon. Sprinkle over dough.
5. Roll up jelly-roll style and seal. Cut into twelve 1-inch slices. Place, cut side down, in a greased 9″ x 9″ x 2″ baking pan.
6. Brush with 1 Tbsp. melted butter.
7. Bake at 350°F for 20–25 minutes. Turn out onto a rack.
8. Combine powdered sugar, vanilla, and milk. Drizzle over warm rolls.

PIZZA CRUST

Makes 2 crusts

1 pkg. dry yeast
2½ cups sifted all-purpose flour, divided
1 tsp. salt
1 cup warm water
2 Tbsp. vegetable or olive oil, divided

1. In large mixer bowl combine yeast, 1 cup flour, and salt.
2. Add warm water and 1 Tbsp. oil. Beat at low speed of mixer for 1 minute, scraping sides of bowl. Beat 3 minutes at high speed. By hand, stir in enough of the remaining flour to make a stiff dough. Knead until smooth, 8–10 minutes.
3. Place in a greased bowl, turning once to grease surface. Cover and let rise until more than double, about 1½ hours.
4. Punch down. Cover and chill until cold, about 2 hours.
5. Cut dough in half. On floured surface, roll each half to a 12-inch circle, about ⅛-inch thick. Place in two greased 12-inch pizza pans. Crimp edges. Brush with remaining oil before adding toppings.

ZUCCHINI BREAD

Makes 2 loaves

1½ cups sugar
1 cup vegetable oil
3 eggs
1 tsp. vanilla
1 tsp. lemon juice
3 cups all-purpose flour
1 tsp. salt

1½ Tbsp. cinnamon
1 tsp. baking soda
2 tsp. baking powder
1½ cups shredded zucchini
½ cup chopped pecans
⅓ cup raisins

1. Combine sugar with oil. Beat well.
2. Add eggs and beat well.
3. Stir in vanilla and lemon juice.
4. Sift dry ingredients together and add to sugar mixture, mixing well.
5. Fold in zucchini, pecans, and raisins.
6. Pour into greased loaf pans. Bake at 350°F for 30–35 minutes.

DOUGHNUTS

Makes 2 dozen doughnuts

1 Tbsp. butter or margarine, at
    room temperature
½ cup sugar
2 eggs
2½ cups sifted all-purpose flour
½ tsp. salt

2 tsp. baking powder
½ tsp. cinnamon
½ tsp. nutmeg
½ cup milk
vegetable oil

1. Combine butter, sugar, and eggs until well blended.
2. Sift together flour, salt, baking powder, cinnamon, and nutmeg. Add to creamed mixture.
3. Gradually add milk. Mix until a smooth dough is formed.
4. Roll ½ inch thick on a lightly floured board. Cut with a doughnut cutter. The less the dough is handled, the more tender the doughnuts will be.
5. Fry doughnuts in deep hot fat (360°F) until golden brown on all sides, turning to brown evenly.

<< Doughnuts

NORMA JEAN'S DOUGHNUTS

Makes 3 dozen doughnuts

2 pkg. dry yeast
¼ cup warm water
⅓ cup butter-flavored shortening
2 eggs
1½ cups lukewarm milk
5 cups all-purpose flour, divided
¼ cup sugar
1 tsp. salt
vegetable oil for frying

1. Dissolve yeast in warm water Stir in shortening until melted.
2. Beat eggs. Add milk. Mix well.
3. Mix together 2 cups of the flour with the sugar and salt. Add to eggs and milk. Place this dough into the remaining flour and work it in until you have formed a big ball of dough.
4. Place the dough in a bowl in a warm place until it has risen to twice its original size. That usually takes about an hour.
5. Turn the dough onto a floured surface and roll out to a ½-inch thickness. Cut out doughnuts with doughnut cutter and place on a floured surface.
6. Let rise again for 30–40 minutes.
7. Drop the dough rings into hot oil and fry on both sides until golden brown. Drain on paper towels.

White Glaze:
    ⅓ cup margarine, melted
    2 cups powdered sugar
    1½ tsp. vanilla
    4–5 Tbsp. milk

1. Add sugar to melted margarine. Mix well.
2. Stir in the vanilla.
3. Add milk one spoonful at a time until the right consistency is reached. Drizzle over hot doughnuts and serve hot or cold.

Note:

    For chocolate glaze, add one ounce of German sweet chocolate with the margarine and melt on slow heat.

FRENCH MARKET DOUGHNUTS (BEIGNETS)

Makes 2 dozen doughnuts

1 pkg. dry yeast
¼ cup very warm water
¼ cup sugar
½ tsp. salt
1 egg, beaten
¾ cup milk
2 Tbsp. vegetable oil
3½ cups flour
½ tsp. nutmeg
oil for frying
powdered sugar

1. Dissolve yeast in water.
2. Add sugar, salt, beaten egg, milk, oil, flour, and nutmeg. Beat well until smooth.
3. Cover and let rise in warm place until doubled. Punch down and knead about eight times. Roll into a rectangle about $1/8$ inch thick. Cut into 3″ x 2″ rectangles. Cover lightly and let rise again about 20 minutes.
4. In heavy skillet, heat oil to about 365°F. Fry two or three beignets at a time until they puff and turn golden brown on both sides. Drain and roll in powdered sugar. Serve hot.

Desserts

HONEY CAKE

Makes 8 servings

During the World War II–years in the South (as elsewhere), sugar was a commodity to be rationed. Our mom had to use coupons from her ration book to buy many items. Shoes for the kids were more important than sugar. She often used honey in place of sugar, or to make it go further.

1 tsp. baking soda
½ tsp. baking powder
2 cups honey
¼ cup sugar
½ cup strong coffee
3 eggs
½ tsp. cinnamon
3½ cups flour
1 cup chopped pecans
7 Tbsp. vegetable oil

1. Add baking soda and baking powder to the honey. Mix until the honey looks white.
2. Stir in sugar, coffee, and eggs.
3. Sift cinnamon and flour together and add to mixture. Mix well.
4. Stir in pecans. Let stand for 10 minutes.
5. Add oil. Pour into paper-lined, 10-inch tube pan.
6. Bake at 325°F for 1 hour.

OUR MOTHER'S CARAMEL CAKE

Makes 10–12 servings

2¼ cups sifted cake flour
2½ tsp. baking powder
1 tsp. salt
1 cup sugar
½ cup light brown sugar

½ cup butter-flavored shortening
1 cup milk, divided
2 eggs
1 tsp. vanilla

1. Sift together flour, baking powder, salt, and sugars.
2. Add shortening and ½ cup milk. Mix well with an electric mixer, approximately 2 minutes on low speed.
3. Add eggs, vanilla, and remaining milk. Beat for several minutes, scraping sides of bowl often.
4. Pour batter into two greased and floured 9-inch cake pans.
5. Bake at 375°F for 25 minutes. Remove from oven and let cool in pans. Use the following recipes for the filling and frosting.

Caramel Filling:
    ¾ cup brown sugar
    ¼ cup sugar
    ½ cup milk

1 tsp. butter, at room
    temperature

1. Combine all ingredients except butter. Bring to a boil and cook on a medium boil until the mixture forms a ball in cold water.
2. Add butter and remove from heat. Cool to warm.
3. Beat until thick and creamy. Spread filling between cake layers.

Caramel Frosting:
    ¼ cup butter
    1 cup brown sugar

¼ cup milk
2 cups sifted powdered sugar

1. Melt butter in a saucepan.
2. Add brown sugar and cook over low heat for 2–3 minutes, stirring constantly.
3. Add milk and continue stirring until the mixture returns to a boil. Remove from heat and cool.
4. Add powdered sugar and mix to the right consistency for spreading. Spread over entire cake.

AMALGAMATION CAKE

Makes 10–12 servings

1 cup butter, softened
2 cups sugar
3¼ cups flour
3 tsp. baking powder
1 cup milk
1 tsp. vanilla
8 egg whites, beaten stiff

1. Cream butter. Gradually add sugar.
2. Sift together flour and baking powder. Add alternately with milk to creamed ingredients.
3. Add vanilla. Beat well.
4. Fold in egg whites.
5. Pour into two greased and floured round cake pans.
6. Bake at 350°F for 15–20 minutes. Cool in pans for 5 minutes and then turn out on rack to cool.

Filling:

- 1 cup sugar
- ⅓ cup boiling water
- 8 egg yolks
- 1 cup butter, softened
- 1 cup chopped raisins
- 1½ cups chopped pecans
- 1 cup flaked coconut

1. Dissolve sugar in boiling water. Set aside to cool.
2. Put egg yolks in the top of a double boiler and beat lightly.
3. Add cooled sugar syrup. Stir well.
4. Add butter.
5. Cook over hot water until thickened, about 30 minutes, stirring often.
6. When thickened, stir in raisins, pecans, and coconut. Mix well.
7. While still hot, spread between layers and on top of cake. Keep the filling over hot water to keep it from getting too hard to spread.

Marshmallow Icing:

- ½ cup sugar
- ⅓ cup water
- 3 Tbsp. corn syrup
- 8 large marshmallows, quartered
- 2 egg whites, beaten
- 1 tsp. vanilla

1. Combine sugar, water, and corn syrup in saucepan. Boil rapidly until syrup reaches 242°F on candy thermometer.
2. As soon as this temperature is reached, stir in the marshmallows until they dissolve.
3. Pour this hot mixture slowly in a thin stream into the egg whites which have been beaten until they hold a peak.
4. Add vanilla. Beat until icing holds a shape.
5. Ice the cake when the cake and the icing have cooled, but before the icing gets stiff.

CARROT CAKE

Makes 10–12 servings

2 cups sifted flour
2 cups sugar
2 tsp. baking soda
1 tsp. salt
2 tsp. cinnamon
¼ tsp. cloves
1¼ cups vegetable oil
4 eggs
3 cups grated carrots
½ cup raisins (optional)
½ cup chopped nuts (optional)

1. Sift dry ingredients and mix together in large bowl.
2. Stir in oil.
3. Add eggs, stirring well after each addition.
4. Fold carrots into mixture with a spoon. (Do not use mixer.) Add raisins and chopped nuts, if using.
5. Pour into three 8-inch, or two 9-inch, well-greased pans lined with waxed paper.
6. Bake at 325°F for 25–30 minutes.

Cream Cheese Frosting:
   8 oz. pkg. cream cheese, softened
   half a stick (4 Tbsp.) margarine, softened
   1 lb. powdered sugar
   2 tsp. vanilla
   1 cup chopped nuts

1. Combine cheese and margarine.
2. Add sugar and vanilla. Mix well.
3. Stir in nuts. Spread on cooled cake.

COCONUT LAYER CAKE

Makes 10–12 servings

2 sticks (½ lb.) butter
1½ cups sugar
4 eggs, separated
¼ tsp. coconut flavoring
¼ tsp. almond flavoring
2⅔ cups flour
2½ tsp. baking powder
¼ tsp. salt
1 cup milk

1. Beat together butter and sugar until fluffy.
2. Add the egg yolks one at a time, beating after each addition.
3. Add coconut and almond flavorings.
4. Sift together flour, baking powder, and salt. Add dry ingredients to creamed mixture, alternately with the milk, beginning and ending with the dry ingredients.
5. Beat egg whites until stiff. Fold egg white mixture into cake batter. Do not beat.
6. Pour batter into three buttered cake pans.
7. Bake at 350°F for 25–30 minutes. Remove layers from oven when they are slightly brown on top. Let the cake layers cool in their pans. Frost with the following icing.

Coconut Icing:
    1¼ cups white corn syrup
    1 tsp. grated orange peel
    2 egg whites
    1 cup flaked coconut

1. Bring corn syrup to boil. Stir in the orange peel.
2. Beat the egg whites until stiff. Slowly pour the syrup mixture into the egg whites. Beat for about 5 minutes.

3. Fold all but one-fourth of the coconut into the icing. Spread between layers of cake as you stack them on top of each other. Complete by spreading the icing on top and sides of cake.

4. Sprinkle top and sides of cake with remaining coconut. Press lightly with your hands to set the coconut to the surface of the cake.

Note:

The coconut that you place on the outside of the cake can be toasted first, which changes the appearance and taste. Place coconut in hot dry skillet and stir constantly over medium heat until coconut browns but does not burn.

LEMON EXTRACT CAKE

Makes 8 slices

I have made this cake every Christmas for years and years. It is delicious, dresses up a dessert plate, and keeps well when stored in the fridge. You can't ask for more than that from a fruitcake.

1 lb. butter, at room temperature
2⅓ cups sugar
6 eggs
3 oz. lemon extract
4 cups sifted flour
½ tsp. salt
1½ tsp. baking powder
½ lb. candied cherries
¼ lb. candied pineapple
¼ lb. white raisins
4 cups pecan halves

1. Cream together butter and sugar.
2. Add eggs and beat well.
3. Add extract and blend.
4. Sift the dry ingredients together and add to the creamed mixture.
5. Stir in fruit and nuts.
6. Pour into two greased loaf pans (9″ x 5″ x 3″).
7. Bake at 300°F for 1½–2 hours.

RUM CAKE

Makes 8–10 servings

This rum cake is very moist and heavy and keeps well in the refrigerator for up to two weeks if well wrapped. All ingredients should be at room temperature before mixing them together.

1 cup margarine at room temperature
2 cups sugar
1 tsp. grated orange rind
½ tsp. grated lemon rind
2 eggs
2½ cups sifted all-purpose flour
2 tsp. baking powder
1 tsp. baking soda
¾ tsp. salt
1 cup buttermilk
1 cup chopped pecans
¾ cup chopped pecans
juice of 2 oranges
juice of 1 lemon
2 Tbsp. rum
½ cup powdered sugar

1. Beat margarine until fluffy. Gradually add sugar. Mix well.
2. Add rinds and eggs, one at a time, beating well after each addition.
3. In another bowl, sift together flour, baking powder, baking soda, and salt. Add flour mixture to creamed mixture, alternately with buttermilk. Beat well after each addition. Fold in 1 cup chopped nuts.
4. Grease tube pan. Place ¾ cup chopped pecans in bottom and along sides of the tube pan. Gently pour batter into pan, trying not to disturb nuts coating inside of pan.
5. Bake at 350°F for 1 hour, or until cake shrinks from pan edges.
6. While the cake cooks, combine fruit juices, rum, and powdered sugar. Bring to a boil, and continue boiling for about 5 minutes. Pour over the cake when you take it out of the oven.

KING CAKE

Makes 10–12 servings

The history of the King Cake is closely associated with the celebration of Mardi Gras in New Orleans. According to an article in the New Orleans Times-Picayune *years ago, the cake originated with the Creole custom of choosing a king and queen on Twelfth Night (or King's Day).*

Because the Spanish historically dominated the area, the traditional celebration of the twelfth day after Christmas, or King's Day, remained part of Creole culture. King's Day commemorates the visit of the three Wise Men to the manger of Baby Jesus in Bethlehem. To the Creoles, it became Le Petit Noel *or Little Christmas. As part of the celebration, lavish parties which lasted until dawn were held on Ash Wednesday. January 6, King's Day, through Shrove Tuesday, or Mardi Gras, became the accepted Carnival season.*

Each week of the season a new king and queen were chosen. The choice was made by cutting the "King's Cake." The cake was large, round, and heavily decorated to represent a crown. A bean, coin, or ring was always baked inside.

At midnight the guests gathered for the cutting of the cake—as many slices as there were guests. If a man found the treasure, he was "king" and would hold up the trinket and announce the name of his queen. If a woman found it, she chose her king by presenting him with a bouquet of violets, which was always provided with the cake.

At some point, the treasure baked inside the cake became a small porcelain baby. Today it is usually a small, hard, plastic baby.

More recently, it has become the custom that whoever finds the baby must give the next party. As more Southern cities celebrate Mardi Gras, the King's Cake's popularity has spread.

1 pkg. dry yeast
½ cup warm water
6 Tbsp. milk
4 cups flour, divided
1 cup butter, melted
¾ cup sugar
¼ tsp. salt
4 eggs
1 small, hard, plastic baby about 1 inch long
corn syrup or icing (see next page)
¾ cup gold-, green-, and purple-colored sugar

1. Dissolve the yeast in the warm water.
2. Add milk and ½ cup flour to make a soft dough.

Continued on next page . . .

3. In a separate bowl, combine the butter, sugar, salt, and eggs with an electric mixer.

4. Add the ball of soft dough and mix thoroughly.

5. Gradually add 2½ cups flour. Place dough in greased bowl and brush top with butter. Cover with a cloth and set aside. Let mixture rise until it is about double (about 3 hours).

6. Knead the remaining cup of flour into the dough and roll it into a rope shape. Place the dough on a greased cookie sheet and form into a round shape, connecting the ends and dampening them with water so they stick together. Cover and let rise for about one hour, or until the dough doubles in size.

7. Bake at 325°F for about 35 minutes or until lightly browned. When the cake is done, raise one side of the cake and put the plastic baby into the dough on the underside of the cake. Decorate the cake by icing it or brushing it with corn syrup and then sprinkling alternating bands of gold, green, and purple sugar.

Icing:
    1 cup powdered sugar
    1 tbsp. milk
    1 tsp. vanilla

1. In a small mixing bowl, whisk together powdered sugar, milk, and vanilla.

2. Allow cake to cool completely before drizzling with icing.

Note:
To color the sugar, put it in a jar with a few drops of food coloring and shake the jar until you have the desired color. You may also use colored icing.

SAM HOUSTON WHITE CAKE

Makes 8–10 servings

¾ cup butter or margarine, at
    room temperature
2 cups sugar
3 cups sifted flour
3 tsp. baking powder
½ tsp. salt

½ cup milk
½ cup water
1 tsp. vanilla
½ tsp. almond flavoring
6 egg whites

1. Cream butter until soft and light.
2. Gradually add sugar and continue beating several more minutes to incorporate as much air as possible.
3. Combine flour, baking powder, and salt. Sift three times.
4. Combine milk, water, vanilla, and almond flavoring.
5. Add dry ingredients alternately with liquid to creamed mixture. Beat well after each addition.
6. Beat egg whites until stiff, but not dry. Fold immediately into batter, blending well. Do not beat.
7. Pour into three greased and floured 9-inch layer pans.
8. Bake at 350°F for 25 minutes. Cool for 5 minutes then turn onto cooling racks. When completely cool, fill and frost with chocolate frosting.

Chocolate Frosting:
    1½ cups sugar
    2 Tbsp. cocoa powder
    ¼ cup milk
    4 Tbsp. margarine
    1 Tbsp. white corn syrup
    ¼ tsp. salt
    1 tsp. vanilla

1. Combine all ingredients except the vanilla in a saucepan and cook over medium heat. Bring to a boil and boil for about 2 minutes.
2. Remove from heat and add the vanilla. Beat until the mixture is of a spreading consistency.

JELLY ROLL

Makes 6 servings

3 eggs
1 cup sugar
5 Tbsp. water
1 tsp. vanilla
1 cup flour
1 tsp. baking powder
¼ tsp. salt
powdered sugar
jelly of your choice

1. Cream together eggs and sugar.
2. Add water and vanilla.
3. Sift together dry ingredients. Add to creamed mixture.
4. Spread dough in a greased and floured jelly-roll pan.
5. Bake at 350°F for 12–15 minutes. Turn out immediately on a towel covered with powdered sugar. Spread with jelly and roll up. Keep covered with the towel until cool.
6. Slice and serve.

CHRISTMAS PUDDING (BOILED PUDDING)

Makes 10 servings

⅔ stick (5⅔ Tbsp.) butter, at room temperature
1 cup sugar
4 eggs, separated
4 cups self-rising flour (use some for tossing with raisins)
1 cup milk
1 cup raisins
grated nutmeg

You will need to have a fabric (muslin) bag about 9 inches wide and 12 inches tall, stitched on three sides, leaving only the top of the bag open. Mom had a drawstring in the top of hers.

1. Cream together butter, sugar, and egg yolks.
2. Add sifted flour to creamed ingredients, alternately with milk.
3. Beat egg whites until stiff peaks form. Fold into batter.
4. Fold in raisins and nutmeg.
5. Pour into fabric bag and tie tightly. After you have poured the pudding into the bag, wet the bag on both sides, and then place it in gently boiling water. Use a large pot, half full of water. Boil pudding for 1 full hour.
6. Allow pudding to cool. Remove from bag, slice, and serve with sauce.

Sauce:

1½ cups sugar
⅓ cup cornstarch
4 cups milk
2 egg yolks
½ cup (1 stick) butter at room temperature
grated nutmeg

1. Combine sugar and cornstarch in saucepan.
2. Add milk and bring to a boil.
3. Beat egg yolks. Add a little of the hot mixture to the yolks, stir well, and then add the egg yolks to the rest of the hot mixture.
4. Remove from heat and stir in butter.
5. Grate a lot of nutmeg and add. Serve warm over sliced pudding.

MISSISSIPPI MUD CAKE

Makes 10–12 servings

½ lb. (2 sticks) margarine, melted
2 cups sugar
1½ cups flour
3 Tbsp. cocoa powder
4 eggs
1½ cups nuts
4 oz. can flaked coconut
1 jar marshmallow cream

1. Cream margarine and sugar together.
2. In separate bowl, sift together flour and cocoa. Add to the creamed mixture.
3. Add eggs one at a time, beating well after each addition.
4. Stir in nuts and coconut.
5. Pour into a 9″ x 13″ pan.
6. Bake at 350°F for 30–40 minutes. Immediately cover hot cake with marshmallow cream and cool before icing.

Icing
   ⅓ cup cocoa powder
   1 lb. box powdered sugar
   1 stick (¼ lb.) margarine, melted
   ½ cup evaporated milk
   1 tsp. vanilla

1. Sift together cocoa and sugar.
2. Add margarine. Mix well.
3. Add milk and vanilla. Beat until smooth. Spread over cooled cake.

FIVE-FLAVOR POUND CAKE

Makes 10–12 servings

This is the best pound cake recipe I have ever found. I have gotten many compliments on it and have shared it with lots people.

2 sticks (½ lb.) butter or margarine at room temperature
3 cups sugar
½ cup vegetable oil
5 eggs, well beaten
3 cups cake flour
½ tsp. baking powder
1 cup milk
1 tsp. coconut flavoring
1 tsp. lemon flavoring
1 tsp. rum flavoring
1 tsp. vanilla
1 tsp. butter flavoring

1. Cream together butter and sugar until light and fluffy.
2. Beat in oil and eggs.
3. In separate bowl combine flour and baking powder. Add alternately with milk to the creamed mixture.
4. Add flavorings and beat well.
5. Pour into a greased and floured tube pan.
6. Bake at 325°F for 1½ hours, or until done. With the cake still in the pan, take a toothpick and prick holes all over the surface of the cake to allow the glaze to seep into the cake.

Glaze:
    1 cup sugar
    ½ cup water
    1 tsp. each coconut, lemon, rum, vanilla, and butter flavorings

1. Combine all glaze ingredients in saucepan. Bring to a boil, stirring until sugar is dissolved. Boil one minute more.
2. Pour over the cake while it is still hot in the tube pan.
3. Let stand 30 minutes to an hour before removing from tube pan.

CREAM PUFFS

Makes 1 dozen large puffs, or 2½ dozen small puffs

1 cup boiling water
pinch of salt
½ cup butter or margarine at room temperature
1 cup self-rising flour
4 eggs

1. Bring water to a boil in a medium-sized saucepan.
2. Add salt and butter. Remove from heat.
3. Add flour, beating rapidly. The mixture will appear puffy.
4. Add eggs one at a time, beating constantly.
5. Drop batter by tablespoonfuls onto a greased baking sheet.
6. Bake at 350°F until puffed and a golden brown—approximately 10–12 minutes.
7. Allow to cool, then slit an opening into the side of each puff and fill with either vanilla, chocolate, or lemon pie filling.
8. When filled, drizzle with melted chocolate chips, or sift powdered sugar over top.

Vanilla Filling:
    ½ cup sugar
    3 Tbsp. cornstarch
    ¼ tsp. salt
    2½ cups milk
    1 tsp. vanilla
    2 Tbsp. butter or margarine at room temperature

1. Combine sugar, cornstarch, and salt in saucepan.
2. Gradually blend in milk. Cook over medium heat, stirring constantly until mixture begins to thicken. Cook for 2–3 minutes more.
3. Blend in vanilla and butter.
4. Chill until firm.

Note:
   Any flavor of pudding mix may also be used to fill the cream puffs. If using a mix, reduce milk from 2 cups to 1½ cups. Cook, cool, and fold in ¾ cup whipped cream.

BASIC PIECRUST

Makes two 9-inch crusts

2 cups all-purpose flour
1 tsp. salt
⅔ cup shortening (butter-flavored or plain) at room temperature
5–7 Tbsp. ice water

1. Place flour and salt in mixing bowl.
2. With fork or pastry blender, blend shortening into dry ingredients until crumbs of a cornmeal texture form.
3. Add 1 Tbsp. water at a time until you can form a non-sticky ball of dough.
4. Place on a lightly floured surface and roll out dough to ⅛-inch thickness. Cut into desired shapes or place in pie plates.

TEXAS BUTTERMILK PIE

Makes one 8-inch pie

3 eggs
1 cup sugar
2 Tbsp. flour
½ cup butter or margarine, melted
1 cup buttermilk
1 tsp. vanilla
8-inch unbaked pie shell

1. Beat eggs slightly. Gradually beat in sugar and flour.
2. Add melted butter. Mix well.
3. Stir in buttermilk and vanilla.
4. Pour into unbaked pie shell.
5. Bake at 325°F for 35–40 minutes, or until a knife inserted in the center comes out clean.

BUTTERSCOTCH PIE

Makes one 9-inch pie

At potluck dinners when I was a child, somebody always brought butterscotch pies. For some reason, they seemed more popular then than now. They are still just as good!

1 cup dark brown sugar, firmly packed
¼ cup water
¼ cup butter at room temperature
1 tsp. light corn syrup
1⅓ cups milk
¼ cup sugar
3 Tbsp. cornstarch
3 Tbsp. flour
¼ tsp. salt
3 egg yolks (reserve egg whites)
9-inch baked pie shell

Meringue:
   3 egg whites
   2 Tbsp. sugar
   ¼ tsp. vanilla

1. Combine brown sugar, water, butter, and corn syrup in saucepan. Cook until the hard-ball stage is reached, 265°F on a candy thermometer.
2. Scald milk in a double boiler.
3. Combine sugar, cornstarch, flour, and salt, and mix thoroughly.
4. Add the milk gradually while stirring constantly until thick and smooth.
5. Add the hot butterscotch mixture and stir until smooth again.
6. Pour slowly over the slightly beaten egg yolks, beating constantly. Place mixture in double boiler and cook another minute.
7. Cool and pour into pie shell.
8. For meringue, beat egg whites until stiff.
9. Fold in sugar and vanilla.
10. Spread over pie and bake until meringue is browned, watching carefully so it doesn't burn.

CARAMEL PIE

Makes one 9-inch pie

1½ cups, plus 2 Tbsp. sugar, divided
¼ cup brown sugar
⅓ cup cornstarch
4 egg yolks (reserve egg whites)
⅔ cup evaporated milk
2 tsp. vanilla
¼ cup butter or margarine
2½ cups milk
9-inch baked pie shell

Meringue:
    4 egg whites
    2 Tbsp. sugar

1. Combine ¾ cup sugar, brown sugar, and cornstarch.
2. Beat egg yolks. Add evaporated milk and vanilla. Mix well. Stir into the sugar mixture. Set aside.
3. Put another ¾ cup sugar into a heavy skillet. Over medium heat, stir constantly until sugar melts and cooks to a golden brown.
4. Add butter and milk. Stir until butter melts.
5. Still cooking over medium heat, slowly pour in sugar mixture and cook until thickened.
6. Pour into a baked pie shell.
7. To make the meringue, whip the egg whites with sugar. Top the pie with meringue.
8. Bake at 375°F for 8–10 minutes, watching carefully so it doesn't burn.

CHESS PIE

Makes one 9-inch pie

This very Southern pie always brings compliments.

3 eggs
1 cup sugar
1 tsp. vanilla
½ cup butter or margarine, melted
1 tsp. vinegar
9-inch slightly prebaked pie shell

1. Beat eggs in mixer until very thick, fluffy, and foamy.
2. Turn mixer to a lower speed. Gradually add sugar.
3. Add vanilla and continue beating.
4. Slowly add melted butter while continuing to beat.
5. Finally, add vinegar. Mix well. Pour into a slightly prebaked pie shell. The mixture should be very foamy.
6. Bake at 325°F for 30 minutes. Reduce heat to 300°F and continue baking until the center of the pie (about the size of a half dollar) is still shaky.
7. Remove from oven. The pie filling will continue to cook in the center after you've removed the pie from the oven. It should form a crisp flaky top and be golden brown in color.

   Chess pie does not need to be refrigerated for the first 2 days after baking it, unless you prefer it cold.

COCONUT CREAM PIE

Makes one 9-inch pie

1 cup whole milk
1 cup evaporated milk
⅓ cup sugar
2 Tbsp. cornstarch
2 Tbsp. self-rising flour
½ tsp. salt
3 egg yolks (reserve egg whites)

1 tsp. vanilla
½ tsp. coconut flavoring
1 Tbsp. vegetable oil
half a can flaked coconut
prebaked 9-inch piecrust

Meringue:
   3 egg whites
   6 Tbsp. sugar
   ½ tsp. cream of tartar
   half a can flaked coconut

1. Heat milks to scalding point over medium heat.
2. Blend sugar, cornstarch, flour, and salt thoroughly in large mixing bowl.
3. Beat egg yolks until lemon colored. Add small amount of scalded milk to beaten egg yolks, mixing well. Add egg-milk mixture back into scalded milk, stirring well.
4. Add a small amount of egg-milk mixture to dry ingredients, mixing well. Repeat until all egg-milk mixture is combined thoroughly with dry ingredients.
5. Cook for approximately 2–3 minutes, or until the mixture thickens. Stir frequently to avoid scorching.
6. Add vanilla, coconut flavoring, and oil. Mix well.
7. Add half can of coconut flakes to batter, stirring well.
8. Pour into prebaked piecrust and top with meringue.
9. To make meringue, beat egg whites until stiff peaks form.
10. Gradually add sugar and cream of tartar, then beat vigorously.
11. Fold in coconut. Stir well and spread over top of pie.
12. Bake at 350°F for about 10 minutes or until golden brown. Cool before slicing.

***Note*:**
   You can add a pinch of baking soda to the meringue while adding in the sugar and cream of tartar, to brighten the flavor a bit.

EGGNOG PIE

Makes one 9-inch pie

1½ tsp. unflavored gelatin
2 Tbsp. cold water
3 egg yolks
⅔ cup sugar, divided
¼ tsp. salt
1 tsp. vanilla
2 Tbsp. milk
3 egg whites
½ cup heavy cream, whipped
3 Tbsp. rum
9-inch piecrust, baked
1 tsp. nutmeg

1. Soak gelatin in cold water.
2. Beat egg yolks. Add ⅓ cup sugar, salt, vanilla, and milk. Cook over very low heat until thickened.
3. Add gelatin to hot custard mixture. Stir until completely dissolved.
4. Beat egg whites until stiff but not dry. Gradually beat in the remaining ⅓ cup sugar. Fold the custard mixture into the egg whites. Set aside to cool.
5. When cool, fold in the whipped cream and rum.
6. Pour into a baked pie shell.
7. Sprinkle with nutmeg and refrigerate until firm.

MARGARITA PIE

Makes one 9-inch pie

4 egg yolks
14 oz. can sweetened condensed milk
⅓ cup fresh lime juice
2 Tbsp. tequila
4 tsp. minced lime zest
1 Tbsp. triple sec liqueur
9-inch graham cracker piecrust
8 oz. container whipped topping
1 lime, thinly sliced, for garnish

1. Beat together egg yolks and condensed milk.
2. Add lime juice and beat for 1 minute.
3. Stir in tequila, lime zest, and triple sec.
4. Pour mixture into pie shell.
5. Bake at 350°F for 12 minutes, or until filling is lightly but evenly set and edges of piecrust are lightly browned. Cool to room temperature and refrigerate.
6. Cover with whipped topping and garnish with slices of lime.

FROZEN MINT JULEP PIE

Makes one 9-inch pie

1⅓ cups Melba toast, crushed
2 Tbsp. sugar
¼ cup butter, melted
1 envelope unflavored gelatin
¼ cup sugar
¼ tsp. salt
3 eggs yolks
1 cup light cream
¼ cup bourbon
2 Tbsp. mint jelly
3 eggs whites
¼ cup sugar
1 cup heavy cream, whipped

1. Combine crushed Melba toast, 2 Tbsp. sugar, and butter.
2. Butter a 9-inch pie pan. Press crumbs firmly onto bottom and sides of pan. Chill.
3. Combine gelatin, ¼ cup sugar, and salt in medium-sized saucepan.
4. Beat egg yolks. Add to gelatin mixture.
5. Stir in cream and bourbon. Cook over low heat, stirring constantly until custard coats the spoon.
6. Stir in jelly. Chill until mixture begins to thicken.
7. Beat egg whites to soft peaks. Gradually beat in remaining ¼ cup sugar. Beat until stiff. Fold egg-white mixture and whipped cream into thickened custard. Turn into crust.
8. Place in freezer until firm.
9. To serve, remove to refrigerator about 2 hours before cutting. Garnish with sprigs of fresh mint just before serving.

PECAN CREAM PIE

Makes one 9-inch pie

1¾ cups milk
¾ cup sugar
½ tsp. salt
3½ Tbsp. flour
2 Tbsp. cornstarch
1 egg, plus 2 yolks, beaten
1 cup heavy cream
2 Tbsp. butter at room temperature
½ tsp. vanilla extract
¼ tsp. almond or lemon extract
1 pecans, chopped
prebaked 9-inch piecrust
4 egg whites
4 Tbsp. sugar

1. Scald milk.
2. Add sugar and salt. Bring just to a boil.
3. In a separate bowl mix together flour, cornstarch, and beaten egg and yolks with the heavy cream. Beat until smooth.
4. Add a little of the hot milk to the egg mixture and blend. Combine both mixtures and cook in a double boiler over hot water until thickened, stirring frequently.
5. Remove and add butter and flavorings. Beat until smooth.
6. Stir in pecans.
7. Pour into prebaked crust.
8. Beat the egg whites until stiff. Add sugar and blend thoroughly. Cover the pie with the egg-white meringue.
9. Bake at 450°F until golden brown. Watch carefully so the meringue doesn't burn.

PECAN PIE

Makes one 9-inch pie

My daughter-in-law Susan, who is married to my oldest son, Richie, was gracious enough to share this recipe with me. On a weekend visit, she served us this delicious pecan pie. It is truly the best that you will ever eat.

¾ cup sugar
1 cup corn syrup
3 eggs, beaten
3 Tbsp. butter at room temperature
1 tsp. vanilla flavoring
1½ cups chopped pecans
9-inch unbaked piecrust

1. Mix the sugar and corn syrup in a saucepan and bring to a boil. Boil for 2–3 minutes. Remove from heat.
2. Pour slowly into beaten eggs, stirring constantly.
3. Add butter, vanilla, and pecans. Pour into unbaked piecrust.
4. Bake at 375°F for about 40 minutes. The pie should be an even golden brown and completely puffed up on top.

PINEAPPLE PIE

Makes one 9-inch pie

2 cups sugar
2 Tbsp. flour
4 eggs
1 stick (¼ cup) margarine, melted
1 small can crushed pineapple
¾ cup flaked coconut
9-inch unbaked piecrust

1. Combine sugar and flour.
2. Add eggs.
3. Stir in margarine, pineapple (undrained), and coconut.
4. Pour into unbaked pie shell and bake at 350°F for 45–60 minutes.

SWEET POTATO PIE

Makes one 9-inch pie

1½ cups sweet potatoes
½ cup brown sugar
¼ cup (4 Tbsp.) butter at room temperature
2 eggs, beaten
⅓ cup corn syrup
⅓ cup milk
¼ tsp. salt
1 tsp. vanilla
1 tsp. lemon flavoring
¼ tsp. ground nutmeg
¼ tsp. ground cinnamon
9-inch unbaked pie shell

1. Boil peeled, sliced sweet potatoes in water until tender. Remove from heat and drain. Mash until smooth and set aside.
2. Cream sugar and butter together.
3. Add beaten eggs. Mix well.
4. Mix in the syrup, milk, salt, vanilla flavor, lemon flavoring, nutmeg, and cinnamon.
5. Add mashed sweet potatoes. Mix well. Pour into piecrust.
6. Bake at 425°F for approximately 10–15 minutes. Reduce heat to 325°F and continue baking for approximately 40 minutes.

Note:

In order not to have the rim of the crust become too browned, cut two strips of foil, each 1–2 inches wide. About halfway through the baking time, remove the pie from the oven and wrap the foil just over the edges of the piecrust. The edges will continue to bake. They just won't burn while the pie filling bakes thoroughly.

RAISIN PIE

Makes one 9-inch pie

Raisin pies used to be called Funeral Pies. An aunt told me there are two likely reasons for that. You often needed to prepare a food item to take with you in a hurry, and raisin pies are made with ingredients that are readily available. Then, too, they keep well without refrigeration.

1 cup raisins
2 cups water
1½ cups sugar
3 Tbsp. flour
½ tsp. salt
½ tsp. cinnamon, *optional*
1 tsp. vanilla
2 Tbsp. lemon juice
1 egg, beaten
1 double-crust, 9-inch unbaked pie shell

1. Wash raisins and soak in water to cover for at least 2 hours. Drain raisins.
2. Place plumped raisins, 2 cups water, sugar, flour, salt, cinnamon, vanilla, and lemon juice in the top of a double boiler.
3. Add egg and mix well. Cook over boiling water for about 12 minutes or until thickened, stirring frequently.
4. Pour mixture into unbaked pie shell. Either layer the remaining crust over the raisin mixture, or cut the pastry into strips and crisscross over the top. Seal edges of crust.
5. Bake at 350°F for about 25–30 minutes, or until crust is golden brown.

OLD-FASHIONED PUMPKIN PIE

Makes one 9-inch pie

1 cup cooked and mashed pumpkin
1 cup sugar
2 eggs
1 cup milk
4 Tbsp. whiskey
1 tsp. nutmeg
1 Tbsp. flour
1 Tbsp. butter, melted
1 tsp. cinnamon
1 tsp. ginger
9-inch unbaked pie shell

1. Combine all pie filling ingredients. Mix well. Pour into unbaked piecrust.
2. Bake at 425°F for 5 minutes. Reduce heat to 325°F. Bake 35 minutes, or until firm.

VINEGAR PIE

Makes one 9-inch pie

3 eggs, slightly beaten
1½ cups sugar
2 Tbsp. flour
1 Tbsp. vanilla
1 stick (¼ lb.) butter, melted
2 Tbsp. vinegar
9-inch unbaked pie shell

1. Combine all filling ingredients. Pour into pie shell.
2. Bake at 300°F for about 1 hour.

WHISKEY PIE

Makes one 9-inch pie

1½ cups sugar
½ cup all-purpose flour
2 eggs
1 stick (½ cup) butter at room temperature
¼ cup whiskey
½ cup semi-sweet chocolate chips
1 cup pecan pieces
9-inch unbaked pie shell

1. Combine sugar and flour in large mixing bowl.
2. Add eggs and butter. Beat until smooth.
3. Fold in whiskey, chocolate chips, and pecans. Pour mixture into pie shell. Place pie shell on a cookie sheet.
4. Bake at 300°F for 40–45 minutes. Let cool before slicing.

DEWBERRY COBBLER

Makes 6 servings

Dewberries are a wild berry, similar to blackberries and used by Southerners in many ways—jams, jellies, and cold drinks, as well as pies and cobblers. At one time the berries were used as a treatment for stomach ailments, the juice was used as a dye, and the roots of the plant were made into a medicine for coughs and fevers.

1¾ cups flour
1 tsp. salt
1 tsp. sugar
½ cup vegetable shortening
3–4 Tbsp. ice water
4 cups dewberries
2 cups sugar
2 sticks butter or margarine
1 Tbsp. melted butter

1. Sift flour, salt, and sugar together.
2. Blend in shortening until mixture is crumbly.
3. Add enough cold water to bring ingredients together while stirring them with a fork.
4. Divide dough into three balls. Roll each out very thin. Line the sides of a 2-quart baking dish with one-third of the pastry. Layer in half the berries, half the sugar, and half the butter (cut into pats). Cut one-third of the pastry into thin strips and place over top of the butter layer. Add layers of remaining berries, sugar, and butter. Cover with remaining one-third of the pastry on top. Make slits in the pastry and brush with melted butter.
5. Bake at 325°F for 40–45 minutes.

APPLE DUMPLINGS

Makes 6 servings

2¼ cups sifted flour
¾ tsp. salt
¾ cup shortening
5 Tbsp. ice water
6 medium apples
½ cup sugar
½ tsp. cinnamon
6 Tbsp. butter
1 cup sugar
4 Tbsp. (half stick) butter, melted
2 cups water
¼ tsp. cinnamon

1. Sift together flour and salt.
2. Cut in shortening with knives or pastry cutter.
3. Sprinkle with the ice water, mixing only enough to make dough stick together. Round into a ball. Let stand a few minutes to make dough easier to handle.
4. On a slightly floured board, roll dough to ⅛-inch thickness.
5. Cut into six 7-inch squares.
6. Peel and core six medium apples and place one on each square of pastry.
7. Combine ½ cup sugar and ½ tsp. cinnamon and fill apple cavities.
8. Top cavity of each apple with 1 Tbsp. butter.
9. Pull four corners of each pastry square up around apple and pinch together at top of apple. Place wrapped apples, pinched side down, 2 inches apart in a 9″ x 13″ pan.
10. For sauce, combine 1 cup sugar, 4 Tbsp. butter, 2 cups water, and ¼ tsp. cinnamon. Pour over dumplings.
11. Bake at 425°F for 40 minutes. Baste apples often with sauce.

BREAD PUDDING WITH WHISKEY SAUCE

Makes 8 servings

4 cups milk
1 cup sugar
1 tsp. cinnamon
3 eggs

2 Tbsp. butter, melted
1 loaf stale French bread, sliced
   thick

Whiskey Sauce:
  1 cup sugar
  1 cup heavy cream
  dash cinnamon
  1 Tbsp. butter

½ tsp. cornstarch
¼ cup water
1 Tbsp. bourbon whiskey

1. Prepare pudding by combining milk, sugar, cinnamon, and eggs.
2. Stir in melted butter. Pour over bread slices and soak bread until all pieces are soft.
3. Butter a baking pan or skillet. Sprinkle a little sugar in the bottom of the pan before adding soaked bread mixture. Layer bread in pan.
4. Bake at 325°F for about 45 minutes or until set.
5. While pudding is baking make whiskey sauce. Combine sugar, cream, cinnamon, and butter. Bring to a boil.
6. Combine cornstarch and water. Add to sugar mixture. Cook, stirring constantly, until sauce is clear and slightly thickened.
7. Remove from heat and stir in whiskey.

OLD-TIME RICE PUDDING

Makes 6 servings

½ cup dry rice
1 quart milk
½ cup sugar
½ tsp. salt

1 tsp. grated lemon rind
¼ tsp. nutmeg
½ cup raisins

1. Combine rice, milk, sugar, and salt. Pour into a buttered 1½-quart baking dish.
2. Bake at 300°F for 45 minutes, stirring occasionally.
3. Stir in lemon peel, nutmeg, and raisins. Continue baking for 1 hour.
4. Serve warm or cold.

FRIED CUSTARD

Makes 8 squares

1 quart milk
¼ tsp. baking soda
3 sticks cinnamon
2 Tbsp. flour
4 Tbsp. cornstarch
1 cup sugar
6 egg yolks, beaten
pinch of salt
1 tsp. vanilla
1 Tbsp. butter
6 egg whites, beaten
1½ cups cracker meal
vegetable oil

1. Combine milk, baking soda, and cinnamon in double boiler. Let the milk come almost to a boil.
2. In mixing bowl, stir together flour and cornstarch. Take 1 cup of hot milk from double boiler. Stir into flour and cornstarch. Beat until smooth.
3. To the batter in the mixing bowl, add another cup of warm milk, 1 cup sugar, and six egg yolks. Beat well.
4. Pour batter into remaining milk in double boiler. Heat until mixture thickens, stirring constantly.
5. Remove from heat. Add pinch of salt, vanilla, and butter. Beat thoroughly.
6. Pour into a greased 8-inch square cake pan. Cool and refrigerate overnight.
7. Cut into squares.
8. Dip custard into egg whites, then into cracker meal. Fry in hot vegetable oil (1-inch deep in pan) until golden brown.

FRUIT FRITTERS

Makes 8 fritters

1½ cups self-rising flour
2 Tbsp. butter-flavored shortening
2 eggs, beaten
½ cup sugar
½ cup milk
1 can fruit pie filling
vegetable oil
sifted powdered sugar

1. Place flour in mixing bowl. Indent center and cut in shortening.
2. In a separate bowl, mix eggs, sugar, and milk. Slowly pour wet ingredients into shortening and flour. Mix together with your hands as you do for making biscuits. Work all of the flour in until you have a stiff dough.
3. Roll out dough on floured surface as you would for a piecrust. Cut into 3-inch squares.
4. Place a spoonful of pie filling in the center of each. Fold sides over, roll up, and pinch edges together.
5. Preheat enough vegetable oil in frying pan to cover fritters. Cook until golden brown on both sides. Drain on paper towels. Dust with sifted powdered sugar when hot.

Note:
   If you bake these instead of frying them, brush the outside of each fritter with melted butter before placing into the oven.

CARAMEL APPLES

Makes 4 servings

4 apples
water to cover
8 Tbsp. brown sugar
4 Tbsp. butter
¾ cup pecans

1. Wash, core, and peel whole apples. Cover with just enough water to cover, and simmer for 10 minutes. Remove from water with a slotted spoon and place in a serving bowl. Reserve cooking water.
2. To the water, add brown sugar, butter, and pecans. Boil for 15 minutes and pour over apples. Serve warm.

Cookies and Candy

ALMOND CRESCENTS

Makes 1 dozen crescents

2 egg whites
8 oz. can almond paste
½ cup powdered sugar

2 Tbsp. flour
chopped almonds, *optional*

1. Beat egg whites until stiff.
2. Fold in all other ingredients. Mix well.
3. Drop spoonfuls of dough an inch apart onto a buttered baking sheet.
4. Bake at 350°F for approximately 20–25 minutes.

NORMA JEAN'S ALMOND COOKIES

Makes 14–18 cookies

1 cup butter-flavored shortening
1 cup sugar
1 egg, beaten
1 tsp. vanilla

2½ cups self-rising flour
half can almond paste
1 Tbsp. water
1–2 cups slivered almonds

Glaze:
1 cup sugar
½ cup water

1 tsp. almond flavoring
1 tsp. vanilla

1. Cream together shortening and sugar until fluffy.
2. Add egg, vanilla, and flour. Mix well.
3. In separate bowl combine almond paste and water. Soften in the microwave oven for 15–20 seconds. Add to creamed mixture. Mix well.
4. Shape dough into finger-sized cookies. Roll each piece in slivered almonds, coating well. Place on greased cookie sheets.
5. Bake at 350°F for about 20 minutes or until a light brown. Remove from oven. Glaze while still hot.
6. Combine glaze ingredients in a saucepan and bring to a boil, stirring frequently. Boil for 1 minute. Spoon the glaze over each cookie while still hot. Cool before serving.

CASHEW CRUNCHY STRIPS

Makes 1½ dozen cookies

¼ cup butter or margarine at room temperature
¼ cup sugar
¼ cup light brown sugar
1 egg yolk
½ tsp. vanilla
1 cup self-rising flour
1 tsp. water
1 egg white
1 cup salted cashew nuts, chopped
1 square chocolate, melted

1. Combine butter, sugars, egg yolk, and vanilla. Mix well.
2. Stir in the flour, one-quarter cup at a time. Place this mixture into an ungreased 8-inch square baking pan and press down with hands.
3. Combine water and egg white. Brush over the surface of the crust. Sprinkle with cashew nuts. Lightly press cashews into the mixture.
4. Bake at 350°F for 25–30 minutes. Let cool in the pan for about 10 minutes before cutting into strips.
5. Remove strips from pan and place on cookie sheet or large plate. Let cool completely, then drizzle melted chocolate over each strip.

Note:
These strips will keep refrigerated for weeks if tightly sealed.

ICE BOX COOKIES

Makes 3 dozen cookies

1½ cups butter or margarine at room temperature
1 cup brown sugar
1 cup sugar
2 eggs
2 tsp. vanilla
4 cups all-purpose flour
1 tsp. baking soda
1 tsp. cream of tartar
1 cup chopped pecans

1. Combine butter and sugars. Beat until very fluffy.
2. Beat eggs until fluffy. Add to butter and sugar mixture. Mix well.
3. Add the vanilla. Mix well.
4. Sift together flour, baking soda, and cream of tartar. Add to the creamed mixture one cup at a time, mixing well after each addition. Stir in pecans.
5. Tear four to five 12-inch waxed-paper strips. Separate the mixture into four to five balls. Shape each ball into a log and place on a piece of the waxed paper. Roll up in the waxed paper. Repeat with the remainder of the balls. Refrigerate the logs of dough overnight or longer.
6. When ready to bake, remove one log of dough and peel off the waxed paper. Cut dough into slices, each about ⅛-inch thick, and place them flat-side down on a greased baking sheet. Repeat process with other refrigerated logs.
7. Bake at 325°F for 10–12 minutes.

MERINGUE SHELL COOKIES

Makes 1 dozen cookies

6 egg whites
½ tsp. cream of tartar
¼ tsp. salt
1½ cups sugar
1 cup chopped pecans

1. Beat egg whites until peaks appear.
2. Add cream of tartar and salt. Beat thoroughly.
3. Add sugar gradually while still beating.
4. Fold in pecans. Do not beat.
5. Place by teaspoonful onto lightly buttered cookie sheet.
6. Bake at 275°F for 1 hour. Remove from pan to serving plate and let cool.

Note:
   Plan to make these when you will be cooking a dish that calls for egg yolks. These cookies make sure the egg whites are not wasted.

MINCEMEAT SQUARES

Makes 8 servings

These are good made with the pear mincemeat recipe found in the Jams and Jellies chapter, on page 312.

piecrust for one pie
mincemeat
melted butter or margarine

1. Roll out the piecrust and cut into 3-inch squares.
2. Place 1 Tbsp. mincemeat in the center of each square. Fold into triangular shapes and press edges together with the tines of a fork. Brush with melted butter.
3. Bake at 400°F for about 12 minutes or until golden brown.

MOLASSES GINGER SNAPS

Makes 8 dozen cookies

Many cooks in the South use sorghum molasses because it is so plentiful. Traditional molasses is made from sugar; sorghum molasses is made from the sorghum plant, which resembles short corn with a dark brown tassel.

In the fall, sorghum is harvested and run through a press to extract the liquid. In the past, these presses were run by mules. As the liquid boils, impurities are skimmed from the top and the liquid turns golden and thickens. It is then strained and is ready to use. Sorghum molasses is lighter in color and taste than regular molasses and is not quite as bitter.

2 cups sugar
1 cup shortening
2 eggs, beaten
½ cup molasses
2 tsp. baking soda
2 tsp. ginger
1 tsp. ground cloves
1¼ tsp. cinnamon
3½ cups flour
sugar

1. In a large bowl cream sugar and shortening until light and fluffy.
2. Add eggs and molasses and beat well.
3. Stir together dry ingredients and add to creamed mixture, a small amount at a time, beating well after each addition.
4. Pinch off dough with your fingers and form into 1-inch balls. Roll in sugar and place on ungreased cookie sheet about 2 inches apart.
5. Bake at 350°F for 15 minutes or until lightly browned on bottom.

NUTTY LEMON SQUARES

Makes 12 squares

15 graham crackers, crushed
3 Tbsp. sugar
3 Tbsp. margarine, melted
2 eggs
2 Tbsp. self-rising flour
¼ tsp. baking powder
1 cup sugar
¼ cup lemon juice, freshly squeezed
½ cup chopped pecans
2 squares chocolate bark

1. Mix together crushed graham crackers, 3 Tbsp. sugar, and margarine. Press into 8-inch square baking dish. Set aside.
2. In large mixing bowl, beat eggs until foamy.
3. Sift together flour, baking powder, and 1 cup sugar. Add slowly to eggs, beating until smooth.
4. Add lemon juice and beat well.
5. Pour mixture into prepared graham cracker crust.
6. Sprinkle pecans over top of mixture.
7. Bake at 350°F for 25–30 minutes. Remove from oven and drizzle melted chocolate over the top. Let cool, cut into squares and serve.

Note:
   The melted chocolate is optional. You may wish to just sprinkle powdered sugar over the top.

OATMEAL COOKIES

Makes 3 dozen cookies

This is a recipe I worked on for years, trying to get exactly the right taste. You can change this by adding chocolate chips, raisins, or cherries. You may substitute the nut of your choice for the pecans.

2 Tbsp. cocoa powder
1 stick (¼ lb.) butter or margarine, softened
¼ cup butter-flavored shortening
1 cup light brown sugar
½ cup sugar
1 egg
¼ cup milk
1 tsp. vanilla
1½ cups all-purpose flour
½ tsp. baking soda
½ tsp. salt
1 tsp. baking powder
2 cups quick oats, uncooked
2 cups pecans

1. In a large mixing bowl, combine cocoa powder, butter, and shortening.
2. Add sugars. Mix well.
3. Add egg. Mix well.
4. Add milk and vanilla. Mix well.
5. In a separate bowl, sift together flour, baking soda, salt, and baking powder. Slowly add to creamed mixture, mixing well after each addition.
6. Fold in oatmeal and pecans. Drop by tablespoonfuls onto greased baking sheet. Press down with fingers to ¼-inch thickness.
7. Bake at 375°F for 10–15 minutes. Allow to cool slightly before removing cookies from the sheet.

***Note*:**
   If you use self-rising flour, don't use baking soda, salt, or baking powder.

PECAN DAINTIES

Makes 1 dozen cookies

1 egg white
dash of salt
1 cup light brown sugar
2 cups whole pecans

1. Beat egg white and salt until peaks form.
2. Stir in half the brown sugar, mixing well. Stir in remaining brown sugar, stirring well.
3. Stir in pecans.
4. Drop by tablespoonfuls onto a greased cookie sheet.
5. Bake at 250°F for 30 minutes.

WEDDING COOKIES

Makes 2 dozen cookies

1 cup butter-flavored shortening
½ cup powdered sugar
2¼ cups all-purpose flour, sifted
1¼ tsp. salt
1 tsp. vanilla
1 cup chopped pecans
powdered sugar

1. Cream together shortening and powdered sugar.
2. In a separate bowl, combine sifted flour and salt. Add to creamed mixture. Mix well.
3. Add vanilla and pecans. Shape into 1-inch balls. Chill for 1 hour before baking.
4. Place dough balls on lightly oiled baking sheet.
5. Bake at 350°F for 10–12 minutes. Remove from oven and roll each ball in powdered sugar while they are hot.

OLD-FASHIONED TEACAKES

Makes 2–3 dozen cookies

Everyone thinks their mother or grandmother made the best teacakes in the world. Ours really did. This is my mother, Jane McQueen's, recipe.

2 lb. bag self-rising flour
2 cups sugar
1 heaping cup shortening
3 eggs
1 whole grated nutmeg
1 tsp. vanilla
1 tsp. lemon flavoring
½ cup whole milk

1. Pour about three-fourths of flour into a large mixing bowl. Indent center.
2. In a separate mixing bowl, combine sugar and shortening.
3. To creamed mixture, add eggs, one at a time, beating well after each addition.
4. Add nutmeg and flavorings to creamed mixture.
5. Add milk and mix well.
6. Pour creamed mixture into center of flour and slowly work into the flour. You will use almost all of the flour. The only way to mix this is with your hands. You can use a pair of surgical gloves if touching the dough bothers you.
7. Form dough into ball and place on a floured rolling board. Using a rolling pin, roll out the dough approximately ¼-inch thick. Cut with a cookie cutter; then place cookies on a lightly greased baking sheet.
8. Bake at 400°F until cookies are lightly browned, about 8–10 minutes. The cookies will be dry if they are overbaked. Test your first pan by baking cookies for 8 minutes. Since all ovens are different, you may have to bake the cookies for a little longer or a little less time.
   These cookies are delicious hot or cold.

THUMBPRINT COOKIES

Makes 1½ dozen cookies

2 sticks (½ lb.) margarine at room temperature
3 Tbsp. sugar
1 tsp. almond flavoring
2 cups self-rising flour

Icing:
    1 cup powdered sugar
    1 tsp. softened margarine
    1 tsp. cocoa powder
    few drops vanilla
    just enough milk to moisten

1. Cream together margarine and sugar.
2. Add almond flavoring.
3. Blend in flour. Mix well.
4. Form into 2-inch balls.
5. Bake on ungreased cookie sheet at 350°F until almost done. Remove from oven and make an indentation on the top of each cookie with your thumb. Return to the oven for a minute or so longer.
6. Combine icing ingredients. Spoon a small amount into each thumbprint indentation.

Note:
    You may use jam as a topping instead of chocolate icing.

CHERRY GRAHAM CANDY

Makes 2 lb. candy

½ lb. (2 sticks) margarine or butter
1 lb. marshmallows
1 lb. crushed graham crackers
1 lb. raisins
1 quart chopped pecans

1 bottle maraschino cherries with juice
1 small can coconut flakes, *optional*
1 tsp. ground nutmeg
1 tsp. ground cloves

1. Melt margarine in large saucepan on medium heat. Stir in marshmallows until melted.
2. Add remaining ingredients.
3. Spoon out on long piece of waxed paper. Shape into a roll and place in the refrigerator for 1–2 hours. When well chilled, cut into ¼-inch-thick slices and serve.
   This candy remains good in the refrigerator for weeks.

DATE NUT CANDY

Makes 24 slices

3 cups sugar
1 pkg. pitted dates
1½ cups milk

1 tsp. vanilla
1 cup chopped pecans

1. Combine sugar, dates, and milk. Cook in saucepan over medium heat until a few drops in cold water form a hard ball (about 20 minutes).
2. Add vanilla and nuts. Beat until stiff.
3. Shape into a long roll and wrap with a damp cloth. Refrigerate until cold and firm. Remove from cloth, slice in cookie-size slices, and serve.

DIVINITY

Makes 2 dozen pieces

2¼ cups sugar
½ cup white corn syrup
½ cup water
dash salt
½ tsp. vanilla
2 egg whites, well beaten
1 cup chopped pecans

1. Combine sugar, corn syrup, and water in saucepan. Place on medium heat until the mixture comes to a hard boil. Reduce heat and stir frequently. Boil until a few drops in cold water form a softball. Remove from heat.
2. Stir in salt and vanilla.
3. Add egg whites, one-third at a time, beating vigorously after each addition.
4. Fold in pecans.
5. Drop by spoonfuls onto waxed paper. Let stand until firm enough to remove. Store in a cookie tin.

Variation:

For holiday color, add a package of raspberry gelatin to the egg whites, immediately after beating them. Then slowly mix into the syrup mixture. You may choose any flavor or any color gelatin you wish.

Note:

Be sure you cook the syrup mixture long enough, or the final mixture will not get firm enough. Divinity comes out to perfection in cooler weather.

OLD-FASHIONED CHOCOLATE FUDGE

Makes 3–4 lb. candy

3 cups sugar
¼ tsp. salt
3 Tbsp. cocoa powder
1½ cups milk
¼ cup white corn syrup
half a stick (4 Tbsp.) butter at room temperature
1 tsp. vanilla
1–2 cups broken pecans (optional)

1. Combine sugar, salt, and cocoa powder.
2. Add milk and corn syrup. Bring to a medium-high boil, stirring often. After 20 minutes, test by dropping ½ tsp. of the mix into a cup of cold water. Repeat until a soft ball forms when hot mixture is dropped into water. Remove from heat.
3. Add butter, vanilla, and nuts, if using. Stir well. Beat until really thick and firm.
4. Pour onto waxed paper to cool. When candy is cool, you can either cut it into squares with a knife or break it into pieces.

CREAM FUDGE

Makes 3½ lb. candy

4 cups sugar
½ cup cocoa powder
¾ cup evaporated milk
¾ cup water

3 Tbsp. butter at room
   temperature
⅛ tsp. salt
1 tsp. vanilla
1 cup chopped pecans

1. Boil together sugar, cocoa powder, milk, water, and butter without stirring until the mixture forms a softball when dropped into cold water (about 20–25 minutes). Remove from heat and let stand undisturbed until lukewarm.
2. Add salt, vanilla, and nuts. Beat well until fudge begins to lose its gloss.
3. Turn out onto waxed paper. Cut into squares immediately and cool.

BUTTERMILK FUDGE

Makes 2 dozen pieces candy

2 cups sugar
1 tsp. baking soda
1 cup buttermilk
1 Tbsp. light corn syrup
1 tsp. vanilla
half a stick (4 Tbsp.) margarine at room temperature
2 cups pecan halves

1. Combine sugar and baking soda in saucepan.
2. Add buttermilk. Let stand 5 minutes. Stir well. Cook over medium heat until mixture comes to a hard boil. Reduce heat to prevent boiling over, stirring constantly.
3. Add corn syrup while stirring. Boil until a few drops form a hard ball when dropped in cold water (about 20 minutes).
4. Remove from heat. Add vanilla, margarine, and pecans.
5. Beat until fudge is no longer glossy.
6. Drop by spoonfuls onto waxed paper. When cool and firm, remove from waxed paper and store in an airtight tin.

EGGNOG FUDGE

Makes 2 lb. fudge

2 cups sugar
1 cup eggnog
1 Tbsp. light corn syrup
2 Tbsp. butter or margarine at room temperature
1 tsp. vanilla
½ cup chopped walnuts
2 Tbsp. semi-sweet chocolate morsels
2 Tbsp. butter or margarine

1. Butter the sides of a heavy 3-quart saucepan.
2. Combine sugar, eggnog, and corn syrup in saucepan. Cook over medium heat, stirring constantly until sugar dissolves and mixture comes to a boil. Cook to soft-ball stage (238°F), stirring only as necessary. Immediately remove from heat and cool to lukewarm (110°F) without stirring.
3. Add 2 Tbsp. butter and vanilla. Beat vigorously until fudge becomes very thick and starts to lose its gloss.
4. Quickly stir in nuts. Spread in buttered 8- or 9-inch square pan.
5. In small saucepan, combine chocolate pieces with remaining 2 Tbsp. butter. Heat until melted. Drizzle over top of fudge.
6. When cool, cut into squares.

PEANUT BUTTER FUDGE

Makes ½ lb. fudge

1 cup sugar
1 cup brown sugar
2 Tbsp. margarine at room temperature
½ cup evaporated milk
1 cup marshmallow cream (or 16 marshmallows)
½ cup peanut butter

1. Combine sugars, butter, and milk in heavy saucepan. Cook to soft-ball stage.
2. Add marshmallows and peanut butter. Stir until thick and shiny.
3. Cool; then cut into squares.

GOLD BRICK CANDY

Makes 5 lb. candy

14 oz. can evaporated milk
3½ cups sugar
2 sticks (½ lb.) margarine, softened
1 pint jar marshmallow cream
3 6 oz. bags chocolate chips
1½ cups chopped pecans

1. Combine milk and sugar in saucepan. Bring to boil. Boil for 10 minutes.
2. While this is cooking, mix all other ingredients together in mixing bowl.
3. Pour milk and sugar mixture over combined margarine, marshmallow cream, chocolate chips, and pecans. Mix thoroughly.
4. Pour into buttered 9" x 13" glass pan. Chill for at least 3 hours before cutting into squares.
5. Wrapped well in foil, gold brick candy will keep indefinitely in the refrigerator.

Note:
   You can use more or less of the chocolate chips, according to your preference. I like to use all three bags.

PEANUT BRITTLE

Makes 2½ lb. candy

1½ cups sugar
½ cup white corn syrup
2 cups shelled peanuts
½ cup water
1½ tsp. baking soda

1. Put all ingredients except baking soda in a heavy saucepan. Cook over low heat, stirring constantly. When peanuts start popping, candy is done.
2. Remove from heat and add baking soda. Stir quickly and pour into buttered 8-inch square pan. Do not stir after pouring.
3. Let cool thoroughly and then break into pieces.

MOLASSES TAFFY

Makes 2½ lb. candy

Molasses is made from boiled sugar-cane syrup. The more it is boiled, the darker and more flavorful it becomes. Molasses taffy was not only a welcome treat for us Southern children, it was entertainment as well. We made a game with it. The more we pulled and twisted the taffy, the lighter and more pliable it became.

4 cups molasses
1 cup brown sugar
½ cup water
4 Tbsp. (half stick) margarine at room temperature
½ tsp. baking soda
⅛ tsp. salt

1. Combine molasses, sugar, and water in heavy saucepan. Cook over low heat, stirring frequently until candy thermometer reads 272°F, or until a small amount of the mixture cracks when dropped in cold water. Remove from heat.
2. Add margarine, baking soda, and salt. Stir just enough to blend.
3. Pour into a large, shallow, buttered pan and allow to stand until cool enough to handle.
4. Butter the hands of all who will help pull the taffy and gather the candy into a ball. Hand everyone a piece of taffy and have them pull the candy, using their fingertips, until it is firm and light yellow in color.
5. When the candy reaches that stage, stretch it out into a long rope, twist it slightly, and cut it with a scissors into 1-inch pieces. Wrap in waxed paper.

PEANUT BUTTER CHEWIES

Makes 20 squares

¾ cup sugar
¾ cup white corn syrup
¾ cup creamy peanut butter

2 Tbsp. butter at room
  temperature
4½ cups cornflakes
1 cup broken pecans

1. Combine sugar and corn syrup in a saucepan. Bring to a boil and boil over medium heat for 1 minute, stirring constantly.
2. Add peanut butter. Mix well.
3. Remove from heat. Add butter. Mix well.
4. Blend in cornflakes and pecans.
5. Press mixture into a 9″ x 13″ pan to cool. Cut into squares, or place by spoonfuls onto waxed paper until cool and firm.

Note:
  You may substitute crispy rice cereal, or any type of unsweetened cereal, for the cornflakes.

PECAN ROLL

Makes 2 lb. candy

2 cups sugar
1 cup brown sugar
1 cup evaporated milk
¼ cup corn syrup

2 Tbsp. butter
powdered sugar
corn syrup for dipping
1½ cups pecans, chopped

1. Combine sugars, milk, and ¼ cup corn syrup. Cook together until mixture forms a soft ball when dropped in cold water (236°F).
2. Remove from heat and add butter. Cool until lukewarm (110°F). Beat until creamy.
3. Turn onto a pastry board dusted with powdered sugar. Knead until firm.
4. Shape into a roll about 2 inches thick. Dip in corn syrup (syrup can be diluted with a few drops of water) and then roll in chopped pecans.
5. Refrigerate until cool enough to slice. Cut into ½-inch slices and serve.

PRALINES

Makes 1½ dozen candies

2 cups sugar
1 tsp. baking soda
1 cup buttermilk
⅛ tsp. salt
2 Tbsp. butter or margarine at room temperature
2½ cups pecan halves

1. Combine sugar, baking soda, buttermilk, and salt in a large saucepan. Cook over high heat until mixture reaches 210°F on a candy thermometer, about five minutes. While mixture cooks, stir frequently, being sure to scrape bottom and sides of pan to prevent sticking. The mixture will foam up.

2. Add butter and pecans. Continue to cook until mixture reaches 234°F on the candy thermometer. (Or test it for the soft-ball stage. Drop a small amount of the mixture into a bowl of cool water. Form into a ball and pick it up. If it flattens instantly, it's ready.)

3. Remove from heat and cool about 2 minutes.

4. Using a spoon, beat mixture until thick and creamy.

5. Drop by tablespoonfuls onto waxed paper and let cool completely.

Jams and Jelly, Pickles and Relishes

To prepare to can any fruits or vegetables, first place canning jars on rack in large pot. Fill pot with water so jars are completely submerged. Bring water to boil and boil for 10 minutes.

Place flat canning jar lids in separate saucepan and cover with water. Bring to boil. Remove from heat.

Let both jars and lids stand in hot water until ready to fill jars. Drain well before filling.

Always wipe the jar rims and threads with a clean damp cloth after filling the jars. Put lids on jars and screw shut. Invert jars for 5 minutes and then turn upright. (You may also follow the water bath method below.) After an hour, check to make sure each jar is sealed. Place any jars that have not sealed in a hot water bath (described below). This should ensure a tight seal.

For a hot water bath, place folded dish towel in bottom of large cooking pot and fill pot two-thirds full. Bring water to a boil; then gently ease the filled jars into pot, making sure that jars are fully submerged. Boil for 10 minutes for pint jars and 15 minutes for quarts. Remove jars from hot water and allow to cool. As they cool, the jar lids should seal.

Successful jam- and jelly-making requires the correct proportions of pectin, sugar, and acid, so be sure to follow recipes carefully. Sugar acts as a preservative and encourages jelling. Even though it may seem that you could do with less sugar, reducing its amount could make the jelly thin and runny. A good rule of thumb is equal amounts of sugar and juice for jelly of a spreadable consistency.

Pectin, found naturally in fruit, aids jelling when combined with acid and sugar in the proper proportions. Some fruits (particularly apples and some berries) are naturally high in pectin and will jell with little or no added pectin. Low-pectin fruits, such as blueberries and cherries, require extra pectin to set up. Since acid is also necessary for jelling, many recipes call for a bit of lemon juice to supplement acid found naturally in the fruit.

CACTUS FRUIT JELLY

Makes 8 half-pints

3½ cups prepared juice (cooked from about 3 lb. ripe fruit)
1 cup water
¼ cup lemon juice
7½ cups sugar
2 pouches fruit pectin

1. Remove thorns and blossom ends from fruit. Cut fruit in small pieces and crush (you can do this in a blender).
2. Place in saucepan with 1 cup water. Bring to a boil, cover, and simmer for 10 minutes.
3. Place in fine cheesecloth (or jelly bag) and let drip. When dripping has almost stopped, press gently.
4. Measure 3½ cups juice into saucepan.
5. Add lemon juice and sugar. Bring to a full rolling boil over high heat, stirring constantly.
6. Quickly stir in pectin. Return to a rolling boil and boil exactly 1 minute, stirring constantly.
7. Remove from heat and skim off foam with a metal spoon.
8. Ladle quickly into prepared jars, filling to within $\frac{1}{8}$ inch of tops. Wipe jar rims and threads. Screw on lids tightly. After 1 hour, check seals.

CHRISTMAS JAM

Makes 5 half-pints

12 oz. dried apricots
2 cups water
20 oz. can crushed pineapple
6 cups sugar
¼ cup lemon juice
1 pkg. pectin
1 Tbsp. butter or margarine
12 maraschino cherries, chopped

1. Chop apricots and place in a bowl. Cover with 2 cups water and soak for at least 3 hours.
2. Drain and place in a heavy saucepan with remaining ingredients. Mix well.
3. Bring to a full boil over high heat, stirring constantly. Boil for 10 minutes. Remove from heat, spoon into prepared jars, and seal.

FIG PRESERVES

Makes 8 half-pints

4 lb. fresh figs
4½ lb. sugar
⅓ cup lemon juice
1 lemon, thinly sliced

1. Wash, clean, and mash figs.
2. Combine figs, sugar, lemon juice, and lemon slices in a heavy saucepan with just enough water to dissolve the sugar.
3. Bring to a boil over medium heat. Continue to boil for about 15 minutes, stirring occasionally. Pour quickly into prepared jars, wipe tops with a clean cloth, and seal.

STRAWBERRY FIG PRESERVES

Makes 5 half-pints

3 cups figs
2 3 oz. pkg. strawberry gelatin
2½ cups sugar
squeeze of fresh lemon juice

1. Wash, stem, and mash figs.
2. Place all ingredients in a large heavy saucepan and bring to a boil over medium heat. Continue to boil for 12 minutes, stirring occasionally.
3. Pour quickly into prepared jars, wipe tops with a clean cloth, and seal.

HOT PEPPER JELLY

Makes 6 half-pints

1½ cups vinegar
¾ cup chopped jalapeño peppers
¾ cup chopped green bell peppers
6½ cups sugar
6 oz. bottle pectin
green food coloring

1. Put vinegar and chopped peppers in blender and chop fine. Pour into saucepan and bring mixture to a rolling boil.
2. Stir in sugar until dissolved. Remove from heat.
3. Strain through mesh sieve. Wait 20 minutes.
4. Stir in pectin and food coloring. Boil for 2 more minutes. Stir. Pour into prepared jars and seal.

LOQUAT JAM

Makes 6 half-pints

3½ cups prepared loquat pulp
⅓ cup fresh lemon juice
6½ cups sugar
3 oz. pouch pectin

1. Select firm, ripe loquats. Wash, steam briefly, peel, and remove seeds. Chop loquats.
2. Combine loquat pulp, lemon juice, and sugar in large cooking pot. Bring to a rolling boil, stirring constantly. Boil for 5 minutes.
3. Remove from heat and add pectin. Skim foam.
4. Ladle into prepared jars and seal.

ORANGE JELLY

Makes 2½ pints

3¼ cups sugar
1 cup water
half a bottle liquid pectin
6 oz. container frozen orange juice
3 Tbsp. lime juice

1. Dissolve sugar in water in large saucepan. Mix well. Bring to a full rolling boil. Continue boiling for one minute over high heat, stirring often.
2. Remove from heat. Stir in pectin, orange juice, and lime juice. Skim off any foam.
3. Ladle into prepared jars and seal with liquid paraffin.

PEAR HONEY

Makes 6 pints

9 cups pears
juice of 1 lemon, or 1 whole lemon
1 cup crushed pineapple
5 cups sugar

1. Grind pears with lemon juice, or lemon (or chop finely in food processor).
2. Stir in remaining ingredients. Cook until mixture is transparent, about 25 minutes.
3. Ladle into prepared jars and seal.

WINE JELLY

Makes 4 half-pints

3 cups Zinfandel wine
  (rosé or sangria wines may be substituted for Zinfandel)
1 box fruit pectin
½ tsp. margarine, *optional*
4 cups sugar

1. Measure wine into large saucepan.
2. Stir in pectin.
3. Add margarine to reduce foaming, if desired.
4. Bring mixture to a full rolling boil on high heat, stirring constantly.
5. Stir in the sugar quickly. Bring to a rolling boil and boil exactly 1 minute, continuing to stir constantly.
6. Remove from heat. Skim off any foam with a metal spoon.
7. Ladle quickly into prepared jars. Wipe rims and screw lids on tightly. Invert jars for five minutes, then turn upright, or follow water bath method for sealing. After jars are cool, check seals.

ZUCCHINI JAM

Makes 6–8 cups

I found this recipe one year when our garden produced a lot more zucchini than our family could eat. I think our friends avoided us that summer because we were always pushing zucchini. Would you believe this jam has become one of our family's favorites?

6 cups peeled and grated zucchini
1 cup water
6 cups sugar
2 Tbsp. lemon juice
20 oz. can crushed pineapple
2 3 oz. pkg. apricot gelatin

1. Cook zucchini in water over medium heat. Bring to a boil. Reduce heat and cook 7 minutes.
2. Stir in sugar, lemon juice, pineapple, and gelatin. Mix well. Return to a boil and cook for 10 more minutes.
3. Pour into hot, sterile jars and seal with paraffin.

CORN RELISH

Makes 7–8 pints

1 Tbsp. prepared mustard
1 quart cider vinegar
12 cups corn kernels
12 cups cabbage, shredded
6 green bell peppers, chopped
6 red bell peppers, chopped
3 cups sugar
3 Tbsp. salt

1. Combine mustard and vinegar in large stockpot.
2. Stir in remaining ingredients. Bring to a boil. Reduce heat and simmer for 30 minutes.
3. Seal in hot sterile jars.

PICKLED PEARS

Makes 6 pints

2 quarts cold water
2 Tbsp. vinegar
6½ lb. firm pears
2½ cups white vinegar
1¾ cups water
2½ cups sugar
1 Tbsp. mixed pickling spice
1 Tbsp. whole cloves
1 whole ginger root

1. Mix 2 quarts cold water and 2 Tbsp. vinegar in large bowl.
2. Peel, core, and cut pears in half. Drop pears into vinegar solution to prevent discoloration.
3. Combine remaining vinegar, water, and sugar in a large stainless steel or enamel kettle.
4. Tie pickling spice, cloves, and ginger root in cheesecloth and drop into the kettle. Bring to a boil.
5. Rinse pears. Add to boiling syrup and return to a boil. Simmer covered until pears are just tender (8–10 minutes).
6. Place pears and syrup into hot sterilized jars and seal. Leave about ½ inch head space in each jar. Process in boiling water bath for 20 minutes. Cool jars and check seals.

TRADITIONAL MINCEMEAT

Makes 6 quarts

1 lb. beef roast
½ lb. suet (hard beef fat)
2½ lb. apples
1 orange
1 lemon
2 lb. raisins
1¼ lb. sugar
1 cup brandy or whiskey
1 tsp. cinnamon
1 tsp. ground cloves
1 tsp. ground nutmeg
½ tsp. ground ginger
½ tsp. salt
½ tsp. black pepper
1 cup apple cider

1. In a Dutch oven, cover beef with water and cook over a low flame for about 3 hours. Render fat from suet.
2. While the meat is cooling, wash and core the apples, slice the orange and lemon, and remove seeds.
3. Grind meat, prepared fruit, and raisins together.
4. Add rendered fat, sugar, and all remaining ingredients, mixing well.
5. Put mixture in a large heavy pot and cook slowly for about an hour, stirring frequently. Add more cider if mixture becomes too dry.
6. Place in hot sterilized jars and seal. Let rest at least 1 month before opening and using.

PEAR MINCEMEAT

Makes 5 pints

7½ lb. pears
1 lemon
1 apple
1 cup apple juice
1 cup vinegar
1 Tbsp. ground cinnamon
1 Tbsp. ground cloves
1 Tbsp. ground allspice
1 lb. seedless raisins
6 cups sugar
1 tsp. salt

1. Peel, core, and grind pears. Place in large, heavy saucepan.
2. Do not peel lemon and apple—quarter each and remove seeds. Chop lemon and apple and add to pears.
3. Stir in juice, vinegar, cinnamon, cloves, allspice, raisins, sugar, and salt. Simmer 2 hours.
4. Pack into hot clean jars and process in hot water bath. Use in pies, cakes, and other desserts calling for fruit filling.

BREAD AND BUTTER PICKLES

Makes 8 pints

Some farmers consulted the Old Farmers Almanac *and checked the astrological signs before planting, grafting, or reaping. Scorpio, Pisces, Taurus, and Cancer were considered earthy, fruitful signs and, therefore, good for planting. Gemini, Virgo, and Leo were barren signs. Aries is considered the "head" sign, and Leo is the "heart" sign. These were considered good for pickling and other types of canning. Some farmers just depended on phases of the moon.*

25–30 medium cucumbers
8 small white onions
1 green bell pepper
1 sweet red pepper
ice water
½ cup coarse salt
5 cups sugar
5 cups vinegar
1½ tsp. turmeric
½ tsp. ground cloves
2 tsp. mustard
2 tsp. celery seed

1. Slice cucumbers and onions as thin as possible.
2. Cut peppers in narrow strips.
3. Combine vegetables. Add enough ice water to cover vegetables. Add salt. Let soak for 3 hours. Drain.
4. Combine sugar, vinegar, and spices and bring to a boil. Add vegetables and bring to a boil.
5. Remove from heat and pour into prepared jars. Seal.

LIME PICKLES

Makes 5–6 pints

7 lb. cucumbers
2 cups lime
2 gallons water
cold water
2 quarts vinegar

4½ lb. sugar
1 tsp. whole cloves
1 tsp. celery seed
1 tsp. mixed pickling spice
1 Tbsp. salt

1. Slice cucumbers.
2. Combine lime and 2 gallons water and pour over cucumbers. Soak 12–24 hours.
3. Rinse well. Cover with cold water and soak for 3 hours.
4. Drain. Place cucumbers in large stockpot. Combine vinegar, sugar, cloves, celery seed, pickling spice, and salt. Pour over cucumbers. Let soak overnight.
5. In the morning, put on the stove. Bring to a boil and boil for 35 minutes.
6. Put in prepared canning jars, seal, and process for 20 minutes in water bath.

SALT PICKLES

Makes 6–8 pints

enough small cucumbers to fill 6 or 8 pint jars
sprig of dill for each jar
garlic clove for each jar
1 quart vinegar
1 pint water
½ cup coarse salt

1. Leave stems on cucumbers. Wash well and pack in sterile jars.
2. Add dill and garlic to each jar.
3. Bring vinegar, water, and salt to a boil and pour over cucumbers.
4. Seal with sterile lids. These cucumbers take about 2 weeks to develop their pickled flavor. Let them rest for at least that long.

<< Salt Pickles

PICKLED OKRA

Makes 4 pints

2 lb. fresh okra pods
4 garlic cloves
8 sprigs fresh dill
4 small hot peppers
2½ cups white vinegar
2¼ cups water
2 Tbsp. salt
1 Tbsp. mustard seed

1. Wash okra. Remove stems and prick each pod with a fork. Pack whole okra pods in sterilized jars. You can position all okra pods with their pointed ends down, or alternate with half up and half down.
2. Place one garlic clove, two sprigs dill, and one hot pepper into each jar. Make sure the jars are tightly packed.
3. Combine vinegar, water, salt, and mustard seeds in a saucepan. Simmer. Pour over okra to within ½ inch of the top of each jar. Seal jars tightly.

WATERMELON RIND PICKLES

Makes 8 pints

4 quarts cubed watermelon rind
1 cup canning salt
1 gallon cold water
1 Tbsp. whole cloves
1 Tbsp. whole allspice
½ tsp. mustard seed
3 sticks cinnamon
7 cups sugar
½ cup thinly sliced lemon
2 cups vinegar

1. Peel watermelon rind, removing dark green and pink portions. Cut rind into 1-inch pieces.
2. Combine salt and water in a large pot. Stir to dissolve salt. Add rind pieces and let stand for 6 hours or overnight.
3. Drain and rinse. Place rind in a large stockpot and cover with cold water. Let stand for 30 minutes.
4. Bring to a boil, reduce heat and cook until tender, about 20 minutes. Drain and set aside.
5. Tie cloves, allspice, mustard seed, and cinnamon sticks in cheesecloth.
6. Combine spice bag, sugar, lemon slices, and vinegar in large stockpot. Bring to a boil and cook uncovered for 10 minutes. Add rind and simmer until transparent. Remove spice bag.
7. Pack hot rind and liquid into hot jars. Process jars in a water bath for 20 minutes.

Game

RAW MARINADE

Makes 1 quart

Use this marinade when you have plenty of time for marinating.

1 bottle (⅘ quart) dry red table wine
¼ cup red wine vinegar
2 carrots, sliced
2 onions, sliced
6 green onions, chopped
½ tsp. whole peppercorns
½ tsp. whole cloves
½ tsp. thyme
1 Tbsp. salt
3 or 4 sprigs fresh parsley, or 1 tsp. dried parsley
1 bay leaf
vegetable oil, *optional*

1. Combine all ingredients. Some cooks pour a little oil on top of the marinade to help seal out the air.
2. Pour over meat, cover with foil, and refrigerate.
3. During the course of the marinating time, turn the meat over several times. Small pieces of meat are usually marinated for 24 hours; larger pieces for 2–3 days. (If the marinade completely covers the meat, turning is not necessary.)

COOKED MARINADE

Makes 1 pint

Use this cooked marinade if you don't have time for long marinating. It should be poured hot over the meat to hasten the flavoring and tendering process.

> 4 bay leaves
> ½ tsp. dried thyme or 4 sprigs fresh thyme
> 4 whole cloves
> 6 whole allspice
> 1 sliced onion
> 2 sprigs parsley, chopped, or ½ tsp. dried parsley
> 2 cups dry red table wine
> ¼ cup brandy

1. Mix all ingredients together in a saucepan and bring to a boil.
2. Pour marinade over meat.
3. Marinate for 4–24 hours, turning occasionally.

BROILED VENISON STEAKS

For those who prefer their steaks rare, try this with venison. Have **steaks** cut thick—not less than 1 inch; preferably 1½ inches.

Rub with **garlic** and brush with **olive oil or butter.**

Broil over hot coals for 8–14 minutes, depending on the thickness of the steaks and the degree to which you want them cooked.

If the steaks have been cut thinner than 1 inch, pan-broil them, searing them quickly on both sides in a heavy, very hot skillet or griddle, just until browned.

BARBECUED VENISON CHOPS

Makes 6 servings

1 Tbsp. dry mustard
2 Tbsp. onion, chopped fine
2 Tbsp. parsley, chopped fine
½ cup butter, softened
6 venison chops, each about 1 inch thick
½ cup lemon juice
½ cup chili sauce
1 tsp. salt

1. Combine mustard, onion, parsley, and butter. Shape into a small roll and chill until firm.
2. Mix together lemon juice, chili sauce, and salt.
3. Grill chops about 12 inches above hot coals. Brush chops often with the lemon juice–chili sauce mixture, turning only once.
4. Cook until done to your taste, about 10 minutes for rare meat. Remove to a heated platter and place a pat of spiced butter on each chop. Serve immediately.

VENISON SAUSAGE

Makes 11 lb. sausage

7 lb. venison
4 lb. pork
⅓ cup salt
4 cloves garlic
2 Tbsp. black pepper
2 Tbsp. crushed red pepper
5 Tbsp. sage
casings for sausage

1. Grind venison and pork together.
2. Blend in seasonings. Mix and grind twice more.
3. Stuff meat into sausage casings or form into patties.

VENISON ROAST

Makes 6 servings

3–4 lb. venison roast
1 Tbsp. salt
1 quart water
2 Tbsp. bacon fat
2 Tbsp. vinegar
2 bay leaves
¼ tsp. thyme
½ cup onion, sliced
1 clove garlic, minced

1. Stir salt into water until dissolved. Soak meat in salt water for 12 hours. Drain and dry well.
2. Place roast and bacon fat in a large ovenproof Dutch oven. Brown over medium heat until meat is seared.
3. Combine vinegar, bay leaves, thyme, onion, and garlic. Pour over meat.
4. Roast at 250°F for 3 hours, basting every 15 minutes with the pan juices.

GRILLED RABBIT

Makes 4 servings

---

1 young 2–2½ lb. rabbit
1 cup vegetable oil
1 Tbsp. celery seed
1 tsp. paprika
2 tsp. fresh thyme, or ½ tsp. dried thyme
½ tsp. salt
½ tsp. garlic salt
2 Tbsp. lemon juice

1. Cut rabbit into serving-size pieces.
2. Combine remaining ingredients. Pour over rabbit pieces and allow to marinate for at least 1 hour.
3. Slowly broil meat over hot charcoal coals for about 30 minutes or until tender. Turn frequently and baste often with marinade.

ROAST RABBIT

Makes 6 servings

2–2½ lb. young rabbit
salt and pepper to taste
1 cup dry bread crumbs
½ cup ground pork
½ cup ground beef
1 egg, beaten
½ tsp. salt
⅛ tsp. pepper
flour
1 onion, chopped
1 carrot, chopped
6 whole cloves
1 bay leaf
2 sprigs thyme, or ½ tsp. dry thyme
2 sprigs parsley, or ½ tsp. dry parsley
1 cup hot water
milk to taste
melted butter to baste
½ cup white wine

1. Wash rabbit and soak in lightly salted water for 1 hour or longer.
2. Dry and rub well with salt and pepper.
3. Combine bread crumbs, meats, egg, ½ tsp. salt, and ⅛ tsp. pepper.
4. Stuff rabbit with stuffing mixture.
5. Sprinkle a little flour over the top of the rabbit.
6. Combine onion, carrot, cloves, bay leaf, thyme, and parsley with hot water. Place mixture in a heavy roasting pan and place the rabbit on top.
7. Cover and roast in a moderate oven, basting frequently, first with milk until about half done, then with melted butter. Before serving, add the white wine to the pan drippings and pour over the rabbit.

SQUIRREL HUNTER'S STEW

Makes 6 servings

2 squirrels
1 cup vinegar
half an onion, diced
1 clove garlic, minced
¾ tsp. salt
½ tsp. black pepper
half an onion, diced
1 clove garlic, minced
3 stalks celery, chopped
2 carrots, diced
½ tsp. oregano
½ tsp. paprika

1. Wash squirrel thoroughly and cut into serving pieces.
2. Combine vinegar, half an onion, garlic clove, salt, and pepper in a deep bowl. Add squirrel pieces and enough water to cover. Let stand for 3 hours.
3. Drain. Place in casserole dish.
4. Brown at 375°F for 30 minutes.
5. Add remaining half onion, garlic clove, celery, carrots, oregano and paprika. Cover with water. Cover the pan and continuing cooking until tender.

PECAN-STUFFED PHEASANT

Makes 6 servings

The pecans in this recipe add additional fat to help keep the bird moist.

2 pheasants
4 Tbsp. butter, melted
1⅓ cups dry bread crumbs
⅔ cup pecans, coarsely chopped
2 Tbsp. flour
¾ tsp. salt
¼ tsp. black pepper
4 Tbsp. butter
1½ cups chicken broth
⅓ cup sherry

1. Rinse pheasants and pat dry.
2. Combine 4 Tbsp. melted butter, bread crumbs, and pecans, tossing together lightly. Stuff mixture into pheasants. Truss to close.
3. Combine flour, salt, and pepper, and lightly sprinkle over pheasants.
4. Melt remaining 4 Tbsp. butter in a heavy skillet and brown each pheasant on all sides. Reserve drippings. Transfer pheasants to a roasting pan.
5. Add broth and sherry to the browned butter and pour mixture over birds.
6. Cover and bake at 350°F for 1 hour. Baste birds with liquid in the pan every 15 minutes. Remove the cover and continue baking for about 15 minutes or until birds are browned.
7. Remove pheasants to a platter and pour drippings over birds to serve.

CREOLE FROG LEGS

Makes 7–8 servings

15 frog legs
3 cups milk
½ tsp. garlic powder
1 tsp. paprika
½ tsp. onion powder
½ tsp. cayenne pepper
dash of oregano
salt to taste
½ tsp. black pepper
½ cup flour
1 cup vegetable oil

1. Skin and clean frog legs well. Place legs in a mixing bowl.
2. Combine milk and garlic powder. Pour over legs. Refrigerate overnight.
3. Pat legs dry. Mix together paprika, onion powder, cayenne, oregano, salt, and black pepper. Sprinkle over the top and bottom of each leg.
4. Lightly flour the frog legs. Heat oil in a heavy skillet and fry until golden brown.

FROG LEGS WITH SAUCE

Makes 4–6 servings

8 frog legs
salt to taste
cayenne pepper to taste
garlic salt to taste
onion salt to taste
paprika to taste
flour to coat legs
¾ cup vegetable oil
6 Tbsp. flour
1 medium onion, sliced thin
2 cloves garlic, minced
16 oz. can tomatoes

1. Skin and clean frog legs.
2. Sprinkle liberally with salt, cayenne pepper, garlic and onion salts, and paprika.
3. Roll in flour.
4. Heat oil in a heavy skillet and fry the legs.
5. Remove the cooked frog legs to platter and keep warm. Reserve ½ cup oil in skillet. Add flour to oil and stir until golden brown.
6. Add sliced onions and minced garlic and cook until soft.
7. Crush tomatoes and add to skillet.
8. Add water to desired consistency and season highly. Return frog legs to sauce in skillet and cook 10 more minutes.

ROAST DUCK

Makes 4 servings

2 ducks
½ cup (1 stick) butter, melted
salt to taste
black pepper to taste
paprika to taste
1 onion
1 apple
2 stalks celery
2 bay leaves
2 bacon strips
hot water

1. Wash ducks and pat dry.
2. Brush with ½ cup melted butter.
3. Sprinkle salt, pepper, and paprika on outside of duck and inside its cavity.
4. Cut onion and apple in half. Place half an onion, half an apple, one stalk celery, and one bay leaf in the cavity of each duck.
5. Place strip of bacon over each duck breast. Place ducks in a baking dish.
6. Add hot water to cover the bottom of dish.
7. Bake covered at 350°F for 2–3 hours or until tender. Uncover during the last 15–20 minutes of cooking time to allow ducks to brown. Ducks are done when a cut between the leg and body shows that the juices no longer run pink.
8. Remove ducks from pan and split in half lengthwise. Discard stuffing before serving.

OVEN-ROASTED DOVES

Makes 6 servings

½ tsp. salt
¼ tsp. pepper
1 cup flour
12 doves
vegetable oil
1 cup green onions, chopped
1 cup chicken broth
1 cup sherry
3 Tbsp. parsley, chopped

1. Blend together salt, pepper, and flour. Dredge doves in mixture.
2. In a heavy Dutch oven, brown birds in vegetable oil over medium heat.
3. When all are browned, drain all but 2 Tbsp. oil from pan.
4. Place doves back in Dutch oven. Add onions and chicken broth.
5. Bake at 350°F for about 1½ hours. After the first 30 minutes, add the sherry. Baste several times with pan juices.
6. Sprinkle with chopped parsley to serve.

CRUMB-COATED ROAST DOVE

Makes 3–4 servings

6 doves
3 tsp. salt
¼ cup olive oil
¾ cup fine dry bread crumbs
½ tsp. crumbled oregano
¼ tsp. black pepper
2 cloves garlic, minced
4 sprigs parsley, finely chopped, or 1 tsp. dried parsley
½ cup water
3 Tbsp. ketchup
3 Tbsp. water

1. Thoroughly clean doves and pat dry.
2. Sprinkle with salt and brush with olive oil. Reserve any remaining oil.
3. Combine bread crumbs, oregano, pepper, garlic, and parsley. Completely coat the outside of each dove with crumb mixture. (Reserve any remaining crumb mixture.) Arrange doves in a large greased baking pan.
4. Pour ½ cup water in bottom of baking pan.
5. Combine ketchup, 3 Tbsp. water, and any remaining olive oil and crumbs. Pour over birds.
6. Cover with foil and roast at 350°F for 2 hours or until doves are tender. Add a small amount of water to the pan if needed to keep birds from baking dry.

ROAST WILD GOOSE

Makes 2–4 servings

1 wild goose
⅓ cup vinegar
1½ cups dry white table wine
juice of 2 lemons
juice of 1 orange
1 small onion, sliced
⅛ tsp. nutmeg
1 bay leaf
2 stalks celery with leaves
3 sprigs parsley, or 1 tsp. dried parsley
salt and pepper to taste
2 apples

1. Wash goose and pat dry.
2. In a large bowl, combine vinegar, wine, lemon juice, orange juice, onion, nutmeg, bay leaf, celery leaves, and parsley. Place goose in marinade and let stand for 3–4 hours, turning frequently.
3. Remove goose from marinade and rub cavity with salt and pepper.
4. Place apples and celery stalks inside goose. Truss goose and place breast-side up in a roasting pan.
5. Sear for 20 minutes at 450°F, then turn goose breast-side down, cover pan, lower heat to 350°F, and continue roasting for 1–1½ hours or until tender. Baste occasionally with marinade and pan drippings.

Index